MYSELF, MY PARTNER

Tony Humphreys
BA, HDE, MA, PhD

Newleaf

PART IV: MYSELF, MY PARTNER

This section deals with issues central to couple relationships:

- ☐ What brings two people together
- ☐ The ideal choice of partner
- ☐ Your choice of partner was perfect
- ☐ Living with the differences between you
- ☐ What happens when two protective worlds collide
- ☐ The wisdom and power of opposites attracting
- ☐ Couple conflict is creative
- ☐ Resolving couple conflict

A major belief that underpins the ideas presented in this book is that individuals never deliberately hurt or neglect each other but that such sad behaviours are the means of protecting ourselves in a world of relationships that too often has left us wounded. The healing of those wounds is a prerequisite to the healing of a troubled couple relationship.

PART V: ENDPOINT

The final part of the book describes how intimate partners relate to each other. This final chapter stresses that intimacy is not just about being emotionally and sexually involved but also entails creating intimacy around physical, intellectual, social, career, philosophical and spiritual needs and aspirations.

PART II

MYSELF, MY PARENTS

There

When I'm here
I am there
for you

When not here
I'm still there
for you

When held near
you are dear
to me

When afar
you're still dear
to me

Whether near
or afar
I'm there

Tony Humphreys

CHAPTER 2

RELATIONSHIPS PAST AND PRESENT

*It is not a question of how a husband and wife
can be equal and alike. But rather it is a problem
of how a couple can be equal and different.*
Pierre Mornell

PAST RELATIONSHIPS/PRESENT RELATIONSHIPS

Your past relationships, particularly those in childhood, are critical
in determining the nature of the relationship that you will
establish with your present-day partner. Adults whose parents
provided an emotionally safe and unconditionally loving home
environment have a deep sense of their lovability and capability,
have a love of life, express all feelings and are not afraid to voice
their convictions. Their relationship with their partners is intimate
and resembles their parents' association with them. These adults
have close friendships with three or four others, and have a
respectful and valuing approach to other people they encounter.
They can accept constructive criticism, tolerate frustrations and
respond to mistakes and failures as opportunities for further
learning. They have an acceptance of and celebratory feeling about
their bodies, their sensuality and their sexuality. Whilst being in
touch with their strengths, adults with good early relationship
experiences are realistically aware of weaknesses and shortcomings. They are true to themselves in their interactions with

partners and others, and they resist conforming, for the sake of acceptance, to the artificial values and expectations of partners and others. Gems of people! Regrettably such adults are a rare breed, because, just as we do, our parents too brought their emotional baggage of insecurities, doubts about their worth, lack of confidence and poor sense of self and others into their partnering and parenting roles.

Past relationships with parents and significant others can vary along a continuum of protective relating ranging from mild to severe neglect. Many of you would have had a reasonable upbringing where conditional loving of a moderate nature was your daily diet. This emotional diet would have left you with some serious doubts about your lovability and capability, and led you to creatively develop the protection of dependence on the approval of others, on physical and social appearances, on academic or work or public performance and on success. Failure would be a dreaded experience for you. Unsureness blocks the path of those who gain recognition, not through their unique and vastly capable self, but through specific behaviours. Chronic insecurity and unsafety creep into your life when you are loved only for what you do and not for yourself. You learn to protect yourself from further hurt and the withdrawal of love that is the consequence of not meeting conditions. In your present relationships with your partner, friends, work colleagues and others you may be cautious, tentative and uncertain of yourself; most of all you may be conditional. This type of relating is most evident in the 'shoulds', 'should nots', 'musts' and 'ought tos' that are a common feature of most couple relationships:

- ☐ You should love only me
- ☐ You should never be late

- ☐ You should see things my way
- ☐ You should never be in bad form
- ☐ You should be successful
- ☐ You should never let yourself down in front of others
- ☐ You should always back me up
- ☐ You should always be kind
- ☐ You should not have friends of your own
- ☐ You should always share things
- ☐ You must not spend time away from me
- ☐ You ought to be there for me at all times
- ☐ You must never say 'no' to me

As you can see, all 'shoulds' and 'should nots' limit you to one end of a continuum of bipolar behaviours. You dare not express, or do, the opposite to the condition imposed for acceptance. Patterns of either controlling and dominating or pleasing one's partner figure frequently in the relationships of adults who themselves had a conditional upbringing.

There are those adults whose past relationships were of a nature that left them bereft of any good sense of self or of others. Their world was one of extreme emotional unsafety in which physical, emotional or sexual abuse was frequent. These people developed strong protective strategies to reduce the daily horror of their lives: withdrawal, aggression, depression, delinquency, compulsive and/or obsessional behaviours, violence, sexual abuse, sexual deviance, alcohol dependence, drug dependence and suicide attempts are some of the consequences of not being loved. Lack of loving is probably the common cause of most human problems.

Adults who have experienced past relationships of such an unloving nature have a deep sense of worthlessness and uselessness. In keeping with such an upbringing, they are highly neglectful of their own welfare and that of their partners, and can be extremely difficult to please. They are strongly self-critical and are hyper-sensitive to criticism. They can be either highly aggressive or extremely passive. They have huge difficulties in forming close relationships. In the relationships they do form they tend to be either possessive or dismissive. Any kind of challenge threatens them. They suffer from continual inner turmoil. Time and time again they protectively drive partners and others from intimacy with them.

It is true that your childhood experiences determine how you relate in present relationships. However, as an adult it is not wise or constructive to continue to protectively blame the past for how you are in the present. If you do that you will remain 'stuck' in your poor sense of self and in an unfulfilling relationship with your partner. You have the opportunity now, as an adult, to find the emotional safety which will allow you to take responsibility for changing how you feel about yourself, to heal the hurts and wounds of past relationships, and to relate in loving ways to yourself and your partner. Finding emotional safety and changing how you are in yourself and with your partner are not easy processes; they demand constant work but the rewards are great.

MY MOTHER/MY FATHER

Do you as a partner ever hear yourself say 'I sound just like my father (or mother)' or find yourself doing things in the same way as your father or mother? Do you find that your intimate relationship repeats that of your parents in certain ways? Maybe sometimes, during arguments with your partner, you shout 'You're just like your father (or mother).' Or maybe you find yourself doing exactly the opposite of how your parents interacted with each other – which can be just as protective. Unless you create emotional safety in yourself and between yourself and your partner, you will probably either repeat or directly oppose the protective ways of relating that existed between your parents. For example, perhaps your parents avoided contact with each other and outsiders; you may now repeat the protective avoidance-of-intimacy pattern or be addicted to intimate contact with others.

The recurrence of the relationship patterns of our parents (or of a parent and a significant other) or the development of opposite patterns of interaction is to be expected. The most obvious reason is that these are the protective patterns most familiar to you. However, experience tells me that there are more profound reasons why these patterns occur. A major purpose of repeat or opposing patterns is to get you as an adult to face the rejecting and other wounding experiences of your childhood, and also to face how you continue the patterns of behaviour you creatively developed during your childhood in order to eliminate or reduce these painful experiences. This perpetuation of protective responses seriously blocks not only your mature development but also your relationship with your partner. As you will see, you are likely to be intimately involved with a person who resembles the parent who most made living an emotionally unsafe experience for you. This situation confronts you once again with the unsafety that was present in your childhood relationship with this parent. But now as an adult, unlike the child who is always a victim of home and other circumstances, you have a chance to redeem yourself from the blocking effects of your parent's relationship with you.

In order to appreciate the wisdom of your choice of partner and the potential maturation that is there for you, it may be of help to answer the following question: what was the nature of the relationship between your parents and their relationship with you that may now be influencing how you are in your intimate relating to another? Generally speaking, relationships tend to be either of an enmeshed or of a more grossly protective nature.

An enmeshed relationship between parents

An enmeshed relationship involves a co-dependence with which each partner colludes. It is primarily protective in nature and, as such, blocks growth in the behavioural areas that threaten either partner's present level of security. The fascinating aspect of enmeshed relationships is how each person chooses a partner who employs opposite protections against hurt and rejection. For example, a father who protects himself by means of dominating and controlling behaviours will be attached to a mother whose protection is to be overpleasing and appeasing. In this relationship the opposing types of protective relating are continually reinforced by his controlling and by her passivity and eagerness to please. Both parents are now living their lives through each other, thereby effectively blocking their own individual growth and the blossoming of their couple relationship. The mother will put up with untold demands, criticism, aggression and irritability in order to protect herself from rejection by her husband and from having to face the responsibility of healing her inner vulnerability. The father will continue to hold his wife responsible for his life so that he cannot be held responsible for any failure or shortcomings on his behalf and, like his partner, will not have to face his own inner turmoil. This relationship will plough along, with many ups and downs, but no significant change will occur until one of the partners finds the personal security and, maybe, outside support to confront the relationship's unhappy and unfair nature.

The influence of an enmeshed relationship between your parents and their individual interactions with you will be evident in your choice of partner and in how you relate to him. My own choice of partner was greatly influenced by how my parents related to each other and to me. In the early years of their marriage my mother (who had been the 'spoilt' child of her family) was overindulged by my father (who had been the 'carer' in his family). I now believe that when my mother became invalided by arthritis in her mid-thirties, my father, after a number of years, invented another protector by opting out and becoming more remote from his wife and his children. Somehow in the complex dynamics of their relationship, my mother transferred her conditional affections to me so that I became the 'carer' that my father no longer wanted to be. This pleased my father enormously. Later on as an adult I chose a partner in life who, at the time, needed caring – so I married my mother. I related to my partner in the ways my father had related to my mother. The double influence of my parents was now present.

Some authors suggest that daughters tend to marry their fathers and sons marry their mothers. There is a lot of truth in this but what must not be overlooked is the influence of the same-sex parent in the choice of partner. From many of my women clients I hear stories of alcoholic and violent fathers which led to mistrust of men, experiences of shame and guilt, and mistrust of self. These women typically either avoided relationships with men or became involved with men exactly like their fathers. But the influence of their mothers was greatly present in this selection in terms of their passivity, self-deprecation and tolerance of abuse. In marrying their fathers, these women were being like their mothers and so the horror of their childhoods was repeated. There is wisdom in this seeming madness. These women now have an opportunity to do what their mothers did not do: assert and act on their right to love and respect, and to leave the relationship if these behaviours are not forthcoming. In this way they confront the mother within themselves. They also confront the father within themselves by no longer colluding with their partners' abusive behaviours.

Similarly, I have worked with men whose mothers doted on them, tying them to their apron strings. Their fathers criticised them for being 'mammy's little boy', 'weak', 'girlish' and so on. These men married women like their mothers who continued the process of doing everything for them. But the influence of their fathers was also present. These fathers had failed to be there for their sons to protect them from overinvolvement with their mothers. The ridicule and criticism dished out served only to increase the very behaviours that their fathers could not tolerate. The sons who now allow their wives to control their lives by treating them like children repeat the collusion of their fathers with their mothers' overprotectiveness. These men have marvellously re-created their parents' relationship in their own relationship with their partners. The task of these men is to assert and act on their right to be in control of their own lives, to believe in their capacity to take care of themselves, and to create an intimate, equal relationship with their partners.

There is another kind of wisdom in having a relationship that repeats that of your parents: it provides insights into your own parents' struggles. In your own difficulties with your partner you witness the personal and interpersonal difficulties of your parents. You begin to see that they were victims of their vulnerabilities and childhood experiences, and that they did not deliberately neglect either each other or you. This experience may help you to move away from the quagmire of blame and feelings of revenge or guilt to the solid ground of taking responsibility for your own healing and the determination that the protective cycle of neglect will stop here with you. In these ways you undo the flawed fatherhood and motherhood of your parents.

Some children develop behaviours dramatically opposed to those of their parents and these opposing responses continue into adulthood. However, the dramatically opposite behaviour adopted may be as extreme as the neglectful parental behaviour that so upset them as children. I recall one woman whose parents were both alcoholics. She had been brutalised by them and had determined very early on as a child never to abide or take alcohol. As an adult she married a man who was the opposite of her father. He was quiet and docile, and never drank alcohol. He died quite young and left his wife with four male children. She did her best for them but when they came into adolescence she lectured them ad nauseam about the evils of drink. She would smell their breath, check their clothing and plot out school routes for them so that they did not have to pass by public houses. If they were ever late she would interrogate them: where were you? who were you with? did you go into that pub? All her sons developed dependence on alcohol.

Similarly, I have helped women who were sexually abused by their fathers and who, as adults, went on to be obsessive about cleanliness and extremely overprotective of their children. They also married men opposite in type to their fathers. These men tended to be undemanding, particularly sexually, and colluded with their wives' overcossetting of the children. These children, as adults, lacked confidence, had no sense of their sexual selves and found it extremely difficult to form intimate relationships. So, the diametrically opposed behaviours of the daughters who were sexually abused led to a different but equally devastating inability to cope with life. There is a golden mean between the extremes of behaviour and that needs to be the healing goal of the adult children of parents whose fathering and mothering were deficient.

Parents not being there for each other

In the enmeshed relationship there are at least some means of gaining visibility through responding to the conditional demands of your partner. But in some relationships there is no way of gaining love, affection and recognition. Despair features prominently in this kind of couple relationship. When there are children to this unhappy union, they too become infected with hopelessness.

Parents in these highly protective relationships may relate to each other in a myriad of ways:

- Frequent open conflict of both a verbal and a physical nature
- Frequent abuse of alcohol, neglect of physical and emotional well-being, dependence on prescribed or illicit drugs
- Possessiveness and overinvolvement with each other that excludes other relationships (even with their own children)
- An exorbitant overemphasis on career development, money, material possessions but no expression of feelings
- Retreat into depression or delusional worlds

I have worked with many men and women who, when they were children, were terrified of the rows between their parents, or sat up in bed at night dreading the homecoming of violent and drunken fathers or mothers. I have also heard stories of children feeling invisible in families because of their parents' overinvolvement with each other and further tales of relentless emphasis on decorum, academic performance, conformity to rules and regulations but never any show of affection. The prime need of human beings is to be loved and cherished. To grow up in homes where gross neglect occurs and no love is shown must be tantamount to being blown out as one blows out a candle. The children of these homes have to develop massive protective strategies to try to reduce the intolerable pain of daily witnessing parents neglecting each other and experiencing similar rejection themselves. They may stay out of home as much as possible or engage in extreme parent-pleasing or try to fight fire with fire by becoming aggressive and violent themselves. They may retreat into fantasy worlds, hallucinations and delusions or they may find solace in being out of this painful world through dependence on drugs and alcohol. They may find protection in physical illness or they may become street children or 'drop-outs'. Some will marry or get involved in relationships in mid-teenage years. Others take to prostituting themselves. They will tend to repeat the relationships of their parents and become involved with partners who are abusive and neglectful. The sad, bitter cycle is repeated. Many social supports and much therapeutic help are needed to redeem these despairing souls.

This book is much more geared towards adults who were victims of an enmeshed relationship between their parents and who can, with some help from friends and some counselling, redeem themselves from the legacy of past relationships. Victims of grossly neglectful homes are in need of long-term dynamic psychotherapy and of considerable social help as well.

Parents and being masculine/feminine

There is a tendency to confuse gender issues with masculine and feminine human characteristics. What makes for a healthy family is not the gender issue of having a male and a female heading the family but the presence of a parent who has a balance of feminine and masculine characteristics. In any intimate relationship there needs to be a recognition that both partners require a balance of masculine and feminine behaviours for each of them to achieve self-reliance and separateness from each other. In troubled relationships between parents, the father may have an overabundance of masculine ways of communicating and the mother a surfeit of feminine ways. Sometimes the converse is the case where the father is more feminine and the mother takes on the masculine role. The children of these liaisons will experience considerable confusion and will probably repeat or diametrically oppose the patterns of their parents. For example, the overprotected male child is deprived of opportunities to develop necessary masculine behaviours such as strength, sureness, drive and ambition, and may have an overbalance of feminine characteristics such as gentleness, softness, abilities to nurture and listen, sensitivity and being in touch with feelings. Likewise the female child who becomes passive, shy, unsure, demure and pleasing – in protective response to her mother's passivity and her father's dominating relationship with her – is prevented from developing some of the more positive aspects of femininity and is blocked from acquiring masculine behaviours. On the other hand, the male or female child who identifies with a tough, aggressive and controlling father will develop many of the more unsavoury aspects of masculinity but will lack the feminine touch. As adults, the task of these children will be to moderate the more undesirable masculine behaviours, to acquire the deficient masculine characteristics and, most of all, to set about learning the feminine side of being human.

From many female clients I have heard tales of fathers who were strict, inflexible and authoritarian and who were unable to give any love, gentleness, emotional support or validation of their daughters' femaleness. Their mothers did not protect them from these overbearing fathers. For these women there was a failure in both fatherhood and motherhood. This is not to say that some good did not come from their fathers' strictness and their mothers' passivity. The fathers provided some stability, order, discipline and structure while the mothers provided restraint, gentleness, kindness, caring and nurturing. Typically, these women were attracted to men who were like their fathers and they acted towards men in the ways their mothers had. Redemption for these women could come only through developing both the masculine and the feminine side of being human and asserting their right to be themselves and to be loved and respected in the couple relationship. To stay with the bitter cycle of how your parents were, sadly, leads only to the reopening of old wounds.

CHAPTER 3

CUTTING THE UMBILICAL CORD

Let me fly, says little birdie
Mother, let me fly away.

Alfred Lord Tennyson

FAMILY TIES THAT BIND

A major block to the development of a mature and enduring couple relationship is where one partner fails to separate out from family of origin and remains tied to one or both parents. Such an unhealthy involvement puts undue pressure on the newly formed couple relationship and very often the other partner begins to feel neglected and rejected. I have worked with many couples where overinvolvement and inability to say 'no' to parents by one person in the couple led to an equally vulnerable partner personalising that behaviour and feeling rejected. (Personalising is where you misinterpret your partner's behaviour as being about you and not about your partner.) These feelings of hurt and rejection can fuel equally powerful feelings of anger, resentment, outrage, jealousy and even revenge. Sometimes these feelings in turn are displaced onto the parents who are seen as taking one's partner away. This displacement is intelligent since it means that the more serious and more threatening confrontation with the partner on unmet needs does not now have to happen. Nonetheless, unless this unhealthy attachment to the family of origin is tackled by the couple it will slowly but surely eat into the core of their relationship.

Separating out from your family of origin can be a difficult process, particularly when you have parents who, because of their own hidden (sometimes, not so hidden) vulnerabilities, lay claim on your life. To collude with their dependence means sacrificing your own independence and freedom as an individual and, possibly, the enduring security of your long-term relationship with your partner. I have worked with sons and daughters of parents who either did not talk to them for months on end or continually nagged, criticised and judged them on their choice of partner. Unfortunately, some of these young people broke under the emotional pressure and let go of their chosen companions. Such parents rationalise that 'it is only for your own good that I'm doing this' but this has a hollow ring to it since there is lack of belief in the son's or daughter's ability to decide for self and there is judgment of the chosen partner. The real issue is that these parents want their children to live according to their values and lifestyle, and are greatly threatened by a prospective son or daughter-in-law that does not match these expectations. Imagine the consternation that can occur when a same-sex companion is brought home! Sadly, some people remain inextricably bound to their parents and do not even attempt to create a relationship with another adult. Such a venture would lead to an intolerable level of rejection which these 'trapped' adults would be unable to withstand. It is safer to stay single and at home.

Separating out from family of origin is not necessarily a physical exodus, even though this is advisable for young adults and is likely to be a matter of urgency for older people. As an adult it is difficult to create your own life space, independence, values and lifestyle while living under the roof of parents or in-laws. Living with in-laws is not to be recommended because the web of enmeshed relating can only too quickly stifle the growth of the young couple relationship. Birds fly the nest to build their own homes and the creation of your own love nest is an important couple responsibility. Many difficulties can emerge in two-generation families and not all of these are experienced by the young couple. When, for example, a young married woman moves in to her husband's family home, she may often feel that the place is not her own. Other issues may arise related to handling your own private space and having an active sexual life. I have known cases where the sexual life of the couple took off after they found their own place to live. Of course, the parents (or parents-in-law) can also have difficulty in adjusting to the new situation and can easily feel threatened by the differences in values, skills, lifestyle and educational level between themselves and their son or daughter-in-law. It is not a desirable mix and would require considerable maturity on the part of both the young couple and the parents to work out successfully the clear boundaries that need to be established around both couple relationships. Matters become even more complex when there are other offspring in the home and more complicated again when the young couple begin to have their own family.

Young couples need all the advantages possible when starting to live together. It is well documented that the first two years of any couple relationship are the most difficult because each partner is learning to adjust to the differences between them. Physical separateness from families of origin is very important for a young couple but the more vital issue is emotional separateness. Your leave-taking of your family of origin can take a number of forms, only one of which is healthy; all the others are the drowning pools of personal and interpersonal development. Naturally, these pools vary in depth and the water in some is muddier and colder.

MAINTAINING THE TIES THAT BIND

The types of leave-taking or separating out from family of origin that maintain dependence are:

- □ no leave-taking
- □ purely physical leave-taking
- □ rebellious leave-taking
- □ enmeshed leave-taking
- □ premature leave-taking.

No leave-taking

This is a sad family situation in which the adult child does not manage to extricate self from the controlling and possessive clutches of parents. These people remain stuck in a childish mode of dependence on parents and dare not make a bid for freedom as the emotional consequences would be far too great to bear. The power, arising from the parents' own vulnerabilities, is awesome, leading to protective feelings of helplessness and powerlessness on the part of the son or daughter. These people would need a coun-terforce (maybe a good friend or therapist) who would provide the support, love and encouragement for them to establish their own independent life-path. They would need considerable help not to be pulled back into the net by their parents' responses to their attempts to extricate themselves. I have helped men and women who were both physically and emotionally abused whenever they tried to gain freedom. Such reactions mirror the depth of the parents' own unresolved problems brought from their childhoods, but to 'cave in' under these reactions would be an act of neglect of self and also of parents. At least in the tide of the emotional turmoil that occurs with the attempts to leave, the parents too have an opportunity to seek the help they need to heal.

Certain characteristics are identifiable in the person who has not separated out from parents:

□ Still living at home
□ Being childish and dependent when in parents' company
□ Being timid and fearful or hostile
□ Conforming to values, morals, wishes and ways of parents
□ People-pleasing or overdemanding
□ Lacking in confidence
□ Having few or no contacts outside of home
□ Having no intimate relationships
□ Allowing parents to dominate or dominating parents
□ Taking responsibility for parents' well-being
□ Being irresponsible
□ Avoiding challenges
□ Being insecure in social and novel situations
□ Failing to confront an unacceptable behaviour for the sake of 'peace and quiet'
□ Being isolated and lonely
□ Lacking ambition
□ Frequently feeling depressed and hopeless

It is important to see that the adults who remain at home with parents are not always docile, conforming and passive but can be aggressive, hostile, selfish, irresponsible and overdemanding. However, both sets of behaviours are indicative of deep dependence and insecurity, and neither will free these adults from their imprisonment. These two sets of behaviours are just two sides of the coin of dependence and failure to separate out from family of origin.

Purely physical leave-taking

There are individuals who physically leave the family – may even emigrate – but who do not achieve an emotional leave-taking. When geographical distance prevents them from returning home, these people may displace their dependence onto friends, workmates and partners. It is as if the new people in their lives become the parents who were not fully there for them.

The insecurity of the person who achieves only physical leave-taking may manifest itself in a variety of ways:

- Being possessive
- Being controlling
- Being overdemanding
- Being jealous of partner's associations with others
- Being easily threatened by changes in arrangements
- Personalising differences between oneself and partner
- Clinging to partner
- Sulking and maintaining silences
- Being hypersensitive to criticism
- Having an unhealthy lifestyle
- Constantly needing to be in partner's company
- Being addicted to alcohol, drugs or gambling
- Overworking

All these characteristics are windows into the emotional, social, sexual, spiritual and physical healing that is needed if this person is to be able to achieve both personal and interpersonal fulfilment.

Rebellious leave-taking

It is not too difficult to recognise rebellious leave-taking. These people leave home under a dust cloud of aggression and hostility protectors that they employed to escape the tyranny of overprotection or domination or extreme neglect. Unfortunately, they in turn have now become conditional or rejecting towards their parents. Furthermore, since they did not come from a climate that nurtured independence and self-reliance, they will continue to seek the approval and acceptance of others; alternatively they may be dismissive of and aggressive towards people who mirror their parents' actions or they may seek the protection of isolation and loneliness. Rebellious leave-takers may put on a tough veneer and pretend they need no one but the truth is very much to the contrary.

The characteristics of the rebellious leave-taker generally take the form of behaviours that 'let out' the rage, hurt, frustration and rejection within:

- Blaming parents for personal vulnerability
- Being aggressive, dominant and narcissistic in relationships
- Being overambitious or lacking ambition
- Being determined to prove oneself or being irresponsible
- Being boastful
- Attention-seeking
- Being possessive and controlling of partner
- Being loud in social situations
- Denying lack of confidence
- Attacking and abusing partner who disagrees
- Rarely if ever going to see parents
- Withdrawing when visiting parents
- Being irritable, moody and volatile
- Being violent
- Not listening to self, partner or others
- Having difficulty in maintaining relationships
- Constantly needing to be in friend's or partner's company

▫ Neglecting personal, physical and safety needs
▫ Drinking alcohol heavily
▫ Being critical, cynical and sarcastic
▫ Acting out by hurting self (banging fist off solid object, cutting oneself, drug overdosing)
▫ Being argumentative

These characteristics are alarm signals to a prospective partner not to commit to such a person until considerable inroads have been made on their emotional insecurities and unresolved hurts from childhood. To believe you can change the person is a protective self-delusion which is a signal of the vulnerability which you need to heal before embarking on an intimate relationship with another. Intimacy with yourself is the guarantee of successful intimacy with a partner.

Enmeshed leave-taking

This is the most common leave-taking of all and is marked by the greatest dis-eases of our society – passivity and conformity. Enmeshment occurs when young adults physically leave the family, establish their own career path, live out on their own and eventually set up home with a partner, but still remain tied to their home of origin. These people return home frequently (whether single or married). They still avidly seek the approval, love and acceptance of their parents and can be extremely upset when these expectations are not met. The relationship with their parents remains more important than their relationships with self and their partners (and later on, children). They allow their parents to continue to live their lives through them and will accept intrusions on their couple relationship. Not surprisingly, their partners are threatened greatly by this enmeshment; they can become defensive and hurt, and feel like second-class citizens. They may rebel against or collude with the enmeshment; either response will not change their partners' protective dependence on their parents. Firm action is required to assert the priority of the couple relationship and the need for strong and clear boundaries around that relationship. If your partner is not ready to meet these reasonable expectations, then you have to see what ways are open to you to try to bring about such a desirable state. You may eventually have to choose to leave the relationship.

The behaviours that characterise the enmeshed leave-taker are ones that 'hold in' the hidden conflicts arising from a poor sense of self, continuing dependence on parents, the perpetual unrealistic expectations of parents and fears of life:

- Being childish and dependent in parents' company
- Conforming to values, morals, beliefs and wishes of parents
- Overpleasing parents
- Being shy, reserved, quiet and passive
- Being manipulative
- Being fearful of mistakes and failures
- Being unable to say 'no' to parents
- Taking undue responsibility for parents' well-being
- Failing to confront on unacceptable behaviours of parents for the sake of 'peace and quiet'
- Failing to establish own independent home
- Allowing interference with, or intrusion into, relationship with partner
- Looking for approval from parents
- Though living away, visiting or phoning home frequently
- Wanting to prove oneself to parents
- Constantly worrying

- ☐ Being perfectionist
- ☐ Constantly putting others' needs before one's own
- ☐ Being dependent on opinions and views of parents
- ☐ Being overconscientious
- ☐ Sulking and engaging in hostile silences
- ☐ Rarely asking anything for oneself
- ☐ Frequently feeling guilty
- ☐ Being easily upset when parents criticise

Premature leave-taking

I have sometimes witnessed this type of leave-taking among third-level students and late adolescents who have left home and taken up jobs. They can suffer severe homesickness pangs, be very unsettled, and have difficulties in applying themselves to study or work. They are still children at heart and have left a home that was either overprotective or overdemanding in nature, neither of which prepared them for the independence needed to take on adult responsibilities. Premature leave-taking can occur where parents expect too much too soon from young people. These young people need the strong security of home and the support of their parents to weather the storms of loneliness and vulnerability that they undergo. When this is not present they often return home and this experience can be a severe blow to their confidence and bid for emancipation. Unless they get a compassionate response and there is an admittance on their parents' part that they had not prepared the ground adequately for their exodus, there is a danger that these young people will retreat totally from the emotional, social and career challenges that pave the road to adulthood.

Clearly, the premature leave-taker is not even remotely ready for intimacy with another. Unfortunately, they can often slip into undesirable liaisons with older adults, who may exploit them for their own protective ends. Sometimes there may be an intense, overinvolved relationship with a kindred soul of their own age, often with an early pregnancy, leading to early marriage and family responsibilities. Neither party to this relationship is prepared for the major responsibilities entailed in this double commitment, and a repeat of the disharmonious relationships of the families of origin is very likely.

The behaviours that characterise premature leave-taking are:

- Frequently feeling homesick
- Feeling confused away from home
- Lacking concentration
- Frequently crying
- Telephoning home on a daily basis
- Going home as often as possible
- Complaining of feeling unhappy and not coping
- Frequently asking for help and reassurance
- Having an overintense, possessive relationship with another
- Making too quick a commitment to a relationship with another
- Frequently missing from class or work
- Neglecting physical needs
- Being withdrawn, moody and easily upset
- Being uncommunicative
- Suffering psychosomatic complaints (headaches, stomach pains, insomnia, chest pains, back pain)
- Refusing to make contact with peers
- Being indecisive

CUTTING THE TIES THAT BIND

The frequency with which the various types of immature leave-taking and the protective reactions that follow are encountered provides some measure of how few families achieve the desirable goal of preparing young adult family members for independence and mature leave-taking. Clearly, the degree of failure to attain this goal varies from family to family. The greater the condition-ality or neglect within the family, the greater the difficulties in separating out and becoming independent. Consequently this immaturity is carried into newly formed intimate relationships. What many young people protectively fail to recognise is that in not separating out from parents and home, not only are they neglecting their own individual development but, ironically, they are also neglecting their parents' personal growth.

Adults who remain tied to their parents often cleverly ration-alise their dependent behaviour with such claims as:

- □ 'My parents need me.'
- □ 'My father needs me to protect him from my mother.'
- □ 'My parents have done so much for me; it is my duty to do the same for them.'
- □ 'My parents wouldn't hear of my leaving home.'
- □ 'My parents would be so upset if I acted differently from them.'
- □ 'It is expected that I go home frequently.'
- □ 'It is easier to put up with my parents' demands.'
- □ 'I feel so guilty when I say "no" to my parents.'

When you analyse these rationalisations, you see that they utterly dismiss the ability of parents to look after themselves and to accept that their children may be different. Do you recognise yourself in any of these rationalisations? In remaining tied to your parents, you weave a wonderful protection against having to take responsibility for your own life and leave-taking from home, but this serves only to maintain and exacerbate the vulnerability not only of your parents but of you yourself. In becoming separate and independent, you show love and respect for both yourself and your parents and you create the solid ground for intimacy with a partner. In remaining entangled, everybody loses out.

It makes it so much easier when parents provide a family culture that fosters self-confidence, independence and a strong sense of self. These parents possess in themselves what they are giving to their children. Parents can lift what can become an intolerable burden from the shoulders of adult children when they let them know that they are quite capable of standing on their own feet and can well look after themselves. It helps enormously when parents communicate to young adult family members that what they want is an enduring friendship with their children and the joy of seeing them set up their own independent lives. When such a family atmosphere is provided, it is easy for young adults to take a mature leave-taking of the family. It is more difficult to take this step when unfavourable circumstances are operating. Nevertheless, once young adults are ready to take on the awareness of their dependence on parents, they have a responsibility to take on the challenges of cutting the umbilical cord, creating their own independent life-paths and establishing intimacy with a partner that is free of intrusions from families of origin. When parents resist this process, the young adult needs to rely primarily on self to cut the ties that bind. A friend or partner can support the painful process but the greater work lies with yourself. Basically, you need to parent yourself in ways that affirm your worthiness, your vast capability, your uniqueness and your right to establish your own separate life.

The behaviours that mark the mature leave-taker are ones from which all who interact with this person emotionally gain:

- Unconditional acceptance of self, parents and partner
- Seeing parents and partner as people in their own right

- Seeing self as a person in own right
- Being caring of self, parents and partner
- Believing that parents can take responsibility for their own lives
- Respecting beliefs, values, morals, religious affiliation and opinions of parents and partner
- Respecting own beliefs, values, morals, religious affiliation and opinions
- Not imposing own beliefs on parents or partner
- Non-conforming
- Being self-directing, independent and self-responsible
- Challenging of self
- Being open to change
- Being spontaneous in expression of feelings, ambitions, wishes and needs
- Enjoying privacy
- Loving life
- Having a healthy lifestyle
- Being decisive
- Creating independent intimate relationships with a few significant others
- Being able to say 'no' to self, parents and partner
- Positively caring when parents are unable to do things for themselves
- Not permitting interference or intrusion by parents or in-laws into own and couple life
- Respecting partner's right to say 'yes' or 'no' to expressed needs

The family, then, can be the nest from which offspring fly in order to create their own independent existence and, later on, if and when they choose, to carry this independence and separateness into an intimate relationship with a partner.

PART III

MYSELF, MYSELF

Me

I am me
and when you
want me to be
like you
you don't see me
nor you

I am me
and when I
want you to be
like you
I do see you
and me

I am me
and when we
want each to be
a me
we do see me
and you

Tony Humphreys

CHAPTER 4

HOW I SEE MYSELF

There are persons who have some parts like me,
but no one adds up exactly like me.

Virginia Satir

You enter a relationship carrying an image of your body, of yourself and of how ideally you should be in a relationship. Depending on how vulnerable your body image and self-image are, and how unrealistic or apathetic your ideals are, you will unwittingly burden the couple relationship with these long-standing personal vulnerabilities. Unless you change how you see your body, yourself and your unhealthy expectations, you are unlikely to see the real person of your partner and even less likely to create an enduring and fulfilling relationship.

HOW I SEE MY BODY AND THE COUPLE RELATIONSHIP

I believe there are very few people who do not have doubts about their physical attractiveness. Having suffered from a hateful rejection of my physical looks, I have deep empathy with anyone who is rejecting of their physical self. Unfortunately, very few of us truly celebrate our own unique beauty. What is far more common is a lack of confidence in our physical looks. The cosmetic industry thrives on this insecurity, as do the alcohol, drugs and cigarette industries.

So many adults agonise over their physical appearance. It can be so exasperating, for example, for a male partner when his companion puts on outfit after outfit complaining 'I look awful', 'nothing looks good on me', 'I look like shit' and no matter what he says, nothing appeases the other's rejection of her physical self. I have worked with both men and women who could not bear to look at themselves in mirrors, who hated catching glimpses of themselves in shop, train and bus windows, and who could not believe that anyone could find them attractive. There are couple relationships where one partner has never seen the other naked and love-making must always be done with the lights out and bedcovers up. Though these men and women are seen as attractive by their partner and others, no amount of declarations of 'I love your body' or 'I find you so attractive' penetrates the darkness of their own repulsion to their bodies. This contradicts the old saying that beauty is in the eye of the beholder. I believe the contrary holds true: beauty is in the eye of the beheld. Only when you have come to an acceptance and appreciation of your own unique beauty are you in a position to internalise affirmation of your body from others.

When people have severe doubts about their physical attractiveness they tend to cling to a relationship because they are convinced that nobody else would find them attractive. In spite of verbal, sexual and sometimes physical abuse, they persevere in the abusive relationship. I recall one woman who at fifteen years of age believed she was, in her own words, 'plain and unattractive'. It came as a complete surprise to her when 'a tall, handsome seventeen-year-old' asked her for a date. It quickly became apparent that he also had severe doubts about his physical appearance (though in conventional terms he was regarded as being a 'fine catch'). He used to pad his jackets to make himself look broader. Morning and evening he spent hours in front of the mirror, looking at himself from every possible angle, before he managed to let himself out of the house. He dressed himself perfectly – not a hair was out of place. They were opposite to each other in that she was shy, quiet and reserved, whereas he always needed to be the centre of attention. However, they were the same as each other in that they both had severe doubts about their physical bodies. He began to show his insecurity by being very possessive of her, extremely jealous and overdemanding. He would accuse her of looking at other men when they were out in social settings and of dressing to attract other men. He would insist she wore longer skirts and buttoned up blouses. In spite of all his controlling and critical behaviours she married him when she was eighteen and he was twenty. The jealousy, accusations, criticism and controlling escalated after the marriage and it was several years later when she came for help for chronic depression. Regrettably, he refused to attend for therapy either for himself or for the couple relationship. She stayed in therapy and eventually made a decision to leave him and find a more fulfilling and embracing relationship.

When a child is born, the wonder, uniqueness and beauty of that child is seen by all. I believe that the child also has an innate sense of her own wonder and it comes as a tremendous emotional shock when that sense of her wonder is not endorsed or is horribly contradicted. In order to survive, the child is forced to suspend her own unique sense of her body and take on the criticisms, the comparisons, the labelling, the physical abuse and the neglect of her body by parents and other significant adults in her life. Later on, peers can add to her having to hold onto the imposed notions that her body is 'fat' or 'ugly' or 'dirty', or that she is 'not as attractive as her sisters or cousins'. For this child to assert that 'I am uniquely beautiful' would only expose her to more ridicule and 'put down' messages, so in order to reduce the hurt and humiliation, she has to retain the body image projected onto her by others. The more people who were involved in destroying her innate good sense of her body, the more difficult it is both as a child and later on as an adult to declare her unique beauty. It is just too unsafe to risk such openness. It is not just the presence of behaviours that take away the child's wondrous sense of her body; the mere absence of holding and of affirmation of her beauty and uniqueness also makes it risky to be open.

Why is it that so many of us doubt our physical attractiveness? It must be that it is much easier for those who are vulnerable to project their own inner hurts, grievances, poor body image and self-image onto the bodies of others because the body is so visible. Children and adolescents who are insecure can be masters of the art of ridiculing another's appearance.

I believe that the body of every human being is uniquely beautiful but what twists and distorts it are the inner feelings of anger, rage, rejection, repulsion, hate, jealousy and apathy. When the sources of those feelings are healed and you come to a celebration of your body, every fibre, sinew, muscle, pore and curve is infected with a shining beauty that no cosmetic or surgery could ever hope to achieve. However, to recover the certainty and security you had as a very young child means removing the high walls of protective concrete blocks that you wisely and steadily built up against the tide of hurtful and painful messages about your body. To redeem your body from the projections of others demands patience, compassion, endurance and most of all love. It is a responsibility that demands your attention since you cannot afford to burden your partner and the relationship with this poor body image. Certainly ask your partner for support, love and understanding but only you can heal how you see your physical self.

The first step in the healing journey is to try to picture yourself as a baby or as a very young child (use a photograph if you wish) and be sensitive to the feelings that arise within you. Do you feel love, awe, tenderness, joy, a wanting to stretch across the years to embrace the loveliness of your child? When you feel these emotions, you have begun your healing journey. Slowly but surely take that child by the hand and lead her through the years, holding onto and continually reassuring her that she is and always was and always will be dear and beautiful to your eyes. Keep returning to this relationship until you and the child merge as one wonderful, beautiful and unique person.

There are other actions that will help you to restore the love of your body:

□ Take daily care of your body
□ Rest your body when it is tired
□ Nurture your body with healthy foods
□ Exercise your body to keep it fit
□ Enjoy and take pleasure in all the sensations of your body
□ Adorn your body in ways that are expressive of your uniqueness and creativity
□ Clothe your body in materials and styles that reveal the inner you
□ Listen to your body
□ Regularly look at, touch and massage your body
□ Talk kindly to your body
□ Regularly affirm your body's uniqueness and beauty
□ Remind yourself that you do not want your body to be like that of anyone else; you totally embrace and accept your own unique body
□ Regularly relax your body

□ Challenge your body
□ Treat your body kindly

These suggestions will help you to establish a close, loving, pleasurable and challenging relationship with your body. When you possess this closeness with your body, you are then ready to share your body with another and to enjoy the contact, pleasure and closeness of his body. This poem captures my views on how to relate to your own body and the body of your partner.

Body

When you want
my body
to be like
another body
I am
nobody

When I want
my body
to be like
some other body
I am
everybody

When I want
my body
to be like
no other body
I am
somebody

HOW I SEE MYSELF AND THE COUPLE RELATIONSHIP

How you see yourself is a highly significant issue because it determines not only the kind of partner you choose but also how you conduct yourself in the relationship and how you see and what you expect of your partner. Many words have emerged to describe the phenomenon of self, the more common being self-image, ideal self and self-esteem. In many ways these concepts fall short of fully comprehending what it means to have a sense of self. For me the concept of self is independent and free of all behaviours; it refers purely to your unique being and includes the other givens of being human: vast intellectual potential, an innate drive to individualise self and an immense presence of worth and goodness. On the other hand the terms self-image and ideal self refer to behaviour – internalised definitions by others of you (self-image) and expectations of how you should be (ideal self).

If as a child you frequently experienced critical, blaming, ridiculing, scolding and 'put down' messages, you may have formed an image of yourself (your self-image) as 'a nuisance', 'stupid', 'inadequate', 'falling short', 'never good enough', 'lazy', 'ugly', 'unlovable' and so on. Through a similar process, when your parents made demands, set high expectations, imposed certain standards of behaviour (for example, cleanliness, tidiness, fairness, honesty, high academic performance, politeness), this formed the looking glass through which you formed an ideal of how you ought to be (your ideal self) in order to gain love, recognition and acceptance from your parents. If there is a wide gap between your self-image and your ideal self, self-esteem difficulties will arise because the likelihood of attaining the ideals is remote. Self-esteem, then, refers to how you feel about the gap between self-image and ideal self. It is easy to see how threatening it may have been for you as a child when your parents, on the one hand, were saying 'you're not good enough' and, on the other hand, were demanding that 'you should never let us down'.

A narrow gap between self-image and ideal self can exist if, as a child, you received messages of 'you're wonderful', 'you're so good', 'you're beautiful', 'you're perfect', 'you're my pride and joy'; however these affirmations were in response to your good actions. What you internalised in response to these messages was that 'I am only "good", "handsome" and "wonderful" when I am behaviourally pleasing to my parents'; you did not associate the messages with your unique person. If the messages were given without behavioural strings attached, then they would have confirmed your intuitive sense of your worth, uniqueness, goodness and vast potential and allowed you the safety to express this good sense of self.

Does this mean that when there is a narrow gap between self-image and ideal self no self-esteem problem exists? I believe that the narrow gap poses as many self-esteem problems as the wide gap. At least when the gap is wide you might have some excuse for not attaining the ideals; however, when the gap is narrow you have none and you will be under great pressure to maintain the standards and ideals set for you and internalised by you. A narrow gap leads frequently to such compensatory behaviours as overemphasis on performance, perfectionism, dread of failure, overwork and addiction to success. When the gap is wide, self-esteem difficulties tend to take the form of avoidance of challenges, passivity, rebelliousness, blaming of others, fear, timidity and settling for an average existence.

In order to attain a sense of your worth, independent of behaviour, you need to rise above and free yourself of the limiting behavioural definitions carried in the trilogy of self-image, ideal self and self-esteem. This is the responsibility of each adult. But the dependence that marks childhood can continue in couple relationships, and the limiting process, whereby each partner defines the other through judgments (how each sees the other) and demands (how each wants the other to be), perpetuates.

As you have seen, your sense of self primarily emerges from how your parents and other significant adults in your childhood years related to you. Depending on the nature of those relationships, you either spontaneously developed a love and liking of self or creatively manufactured a subconscious protective self-image and ideal self in order to reduce experiences of hurt and rejection. It is these protective self-perceptions that you as an adult are likely to bring into your intimate relationship with another. However, as an adult you must take responsibility for healing the wounds that led to having protected perceptions of self rather than place that emotional baggage on the back of the couple relationship. Certainly, seek support and resources in the relationship for your individual healing process but do not burden your partner with unresolved emotional issues from your childhood. Attempt to let go of the protective ways you see yourself and move towards an open acceptance and wonderment of self. Before examining how this may be done, it may help you to understand how your present view of yourself is necessary, clever, creative and protective and to see what protective strategies you employ in defining yourself.

SELF-IMAGE AND IDEAL SELF ARE PROTECTIVE FORCES

I recall very early on as a child discovering that being the 'goodie-good' protected me from rejection and gained me recognition even if this was conditional. My mother was an invalid and I was able to gain her acceptance by being the carer. I also found that by taking on that responsibility, I relieved my father of it and so found a way to gain his acceptance. The problem was that once I had intuitively adopted these survival strategies, I was obliged to keep them up because any straying from these obligations resulted in withdrawal by my mother and hostility from my father. Being the carer then became an integral part of my ideal self and it took me many years as an adult to change that protective means of seeing myself. I also now know it was vital that I saw myself in that way as a child because it protected me from invisibility and rejection. Nonetheless, it was a conditional way of seeing myself and as long as that remained there was no hope of establishing a secure, independent sense of myself (and of others). There was a myth in my family that 'Tony can always take care of himself.' What a wonderful protector this was for my family because as long as the myth was maintained, the family had a reliable cornerstone to fall back on. Not surprisingly, I put tremendous pressure on myself to live up to those expectations. For much of my early adult years I maintained this idealistic image of myself. Look at the professions I entered – priesthood, primary and secondary teaching, therapy – all 'caring' professions! In my relationships with women I found that I employed my caring image as a means of initiating and keeping the woman's interest in the relationship. For every rescuer there are many waiting to be saved, and I found no shortage of partners who needed rescuing.

This role did not develop, however, until I had healed a major painful aspect of my self-image concerning my physical self. Due to messages about my physical appearance from significant female relatives in my early life, I learned to regard myself as ugly and unattractive. This was wise of me because it protected me from taking any risks with women and thereby offset any possibility of further rejection experiences of my physical self. I believe that my entering a seminary served two protective purposes: it gave me an honourable way of relinquishing my 'saviour role' in the family and it removed me from the presence of women. Several years later when I decided to leave the monastery, I spent many unhappy years hiding away in corners of university lecture rooms so that I did not have to interact with women. I buried myself in work and study, and felt too vulnerable to form a liaison with a woman. A fortunate experience with a woman several years older than myself, who persisted in her attentions towards me, broke through my web of protection. I have never forgotten her love of me and, even though she died within a year of our relationship, her presence remains strong within me. Of course, I did not suddenly come to like myself, but what a tremendous experience it was for me to discover a woman who wanted me emotionally and, wonder of wonders, physically and sexually as well. Later on, as part of my training as a therapist, where self-analysis is essential, I began to let go of the image of myself as physically unattractive and learned to accept my own unique beauty. There are times that I still struggle with this issue but it has ceased to be a big factor influencing my relationships with women. Similarly, I have let go of my 'carer' image and now sincerely try to be spontaneous and free in my contact with others and not manipulate them into loving me through my rescuing skills. Nevertheless, those rescuing skills provided me with the basis of how to care for myself and others. In the past I had not cared for myself since to do so would have risked the response of 'you're so selfish' and tarnished the caring image I projected.

Human beings are absolutely marvellous at developing images of themselves that protect against rejection and ideals that fit in with the expectations of others. Children are masters of this art. Children within conditional or deeply troubled families can develop any one or a combination of the following ways of protecting themselves.

IDEAL IMAGE PROTECTORS

- □ The goodie-good child
- □ The perfectionist
- □ The funny child
- □ The sports fanatic
- □ The beautiful/handsome child
- □ The bookworm
- □ The ever-so-pleasing child
- □ The compliant child
- □ The little professor
- □ The little actress/actor
- □ The hard-working child
- □ The artistic child
- □ The little nurse
- □ The little doctor
- □ The little saint
- □ The lovable rogue
- □ The athlete
- □ The 'natural' sports player

SELF-IMAGE PROTECTORS

- □ 'I'm wonderful.'
- □ 'I'm the best at everything.'
- □ 'I'm a loser.'
- □ 'I'm ugly.'
- □ 'I'm stupid.'
- □ 'I'm cleverer than anyone else.'
- □ 'I'm timid and shy.'
- □ 'I'm fearful and nervous.'
- □ 'I'm a loner.'
- □ 'I'm coy.'
- □ 'I'm difficult.'
- □ 'I'm aggressive.'
- □ 'I'm sickly.'
- □ 'I'm useless.'
- □ 'I'm worthless.'
- □ 'I'm weak.'
- □ 'I'm overcautious.'

The list is endless and the more pluralist society becomes, the more ways that children and adults have of developing protective images and ideals for self. A protective ideal self is where you match how you see yourself with the expectations of the significant adults in your life, particularly your parents. You know if you step outside the bounds of this protective ideal self, you are at risk of ridicule, criticism and rejection. How often have you heard the phrases 'that's not a bit like our child' or 'that's very uncharacteristic of her' or 'he doesn't seem like himself at all today'. Children also know that the boundaries around how they see themselves are established by how love is given within the family and when such nurturance may be withdrawn. In relationships that are emotionally threatening children and adults alike devise protective self-image strategies in order to minimise experiences of hurt and rejection. Aggression and unco-operativeness become means of controlling parents and partners who tend to use love as a weapon. Equally, fear, timidity, depression and overcautiousness are means to reduce harsh treatment by another. Children learn early on that it is safe to act only in particular ways and these actions determine how you begin to see yourself and how you expect others to see you. As a young adult you will continue to maintain the same protective self-image and ideals until you feel it is safe to be different or, indeed, truly yourself in certain people's company. People who are generally timid and shy may become the life and soul of an interaction when in the company of others who do not set limits or conditions to their acceptance of them. A more mature place to be is where your own acceptance of yourself is not changed or diluted because other people expect you to behave differently. Whilst you respect their differences, you are determined to be your own person.

I recall working with a married man who worked in his father's construction firm. His father and brother were constantly criti-cising him for being overcautious, timid and fearful. His wife tended to dominate and control him. I felt his image of himself as being overcautious, timid and fearful was a great strength and not at all the weakness that his father, brother and wife were judging it to be. When I asked him 'tell me how your father was with you when you were a child?' he told me 'he was physically violent and hyper-critical'. I then pointed out to him how creative he had been in developing the protective self-image of extreme cautiousness, timidity and fearfulness. The overcautiousness reduced the possibility of the most traumatic experience of all for a child – the withdrawal of love because of poor performance. Because for this man the withdrawal of love was frequently accompanied by a physical beating, the need to find effective means of protection was paramount. When you do things slowly and carefully, you are less likely to make mistakes and so my client cleverly reduced the incidences of failure that drew his father's wrath and rejection. It is the lesser of two evils to risk disapproval for being slow rather than rejection and physical abuse for mistakes and failures. Seeing and projecting himself as timid and fearful were further ingenious strategies to lessen the hurts in his life. When children or adults are fearful, shy and timid, you tend to tiptoe around them and you certainly do not shout and roar at them. My client had used these means to soften his father's approach to him. Until he developed a deep acceptance of himself and an independence of his father and wife, it was necessary for him to retain his protective self-image.

The protective self-image and ideal self you developed as a child may well be the emotional baggage you will carry into your adult relationships. It is important that you now attempt to recognise the self-image and ideal self and the other protective devices you developed to reduce experiences of hurt, and that you discover whether you are continuing these protective strategies of old or developing new ones in your relationship with your partner. A further question to consider is: what are the judgments and expectations your partner makes of you and do you feel free to meet or not meet these definitions and expectations? If to the latter your answer is 'no', then you will find that you bend your self-image and ideal self to meet your partner's demands. There is

quite a difference between feeling you have choice about responding to your partner's needs and feeling obligated to meet them. In
the latter case you are taking responsibility for your partner and
abrogating it for yourself. You take responsibility for self when you
check with yourself whether your partner's judgments and demands
fit in with your values and ways and how you are feeling, and you
then sensitively, but clearly, communicate your honest and open
response while considering the urgency and the importance of the
needs expressed by your partner.

The answers I would have given to these questions in the early
days of my own marriage are set out below.

OLD SELF-IMAGE AND IDEAL SELF STRATEGIES BROUGHT INTO RELATIONSHIPS

☐ Being the 'goodie-good' child

☐ Being the carer

☐ Being responsible for other family members

☐ Non-assertiveness

☐ Suspending expression of my own needs

☐ Being oversensitive to criticism

☐ Being quick-tempered

☐ Hating my physical self

☐ Being the peacemaker

☐ Wanting to not cause hurt

OTHER PROTECTIVE DEVICES BROUGHT INTO RELATIONSHIPS

☐ Avoidance of social situations

☐ Staying in home rather than going out

☐ Tendency to sulk and withdraw

☐ Fearful of doing the wrong thing

☐ Aggressive

→

STRATEGIES PERPETUATING IN MY RELATIONSHIP WITH MY PARTNER

- ☐ Being the carer, but to a far lesser degree
- ☐ Taking responsibility for my partner, but less so
- ☐ Still some difficulty in expressing my own needs
- ☐ Still sensitive to criticism, but less so
- ☐ Still can become irritable, but generally far more easy-going
- ☐ Fearful of hurting my partner
- ☐ Some avoidance of conflict

MY PARTNER'S EXPECTATIONS OF ME

- ☐ Be the carer
- ☐ Be responsible
- ☐ See her needs only
- ☐ Be there for her at all times
- ☐ Not be angry
- ☐ Not see things differently to her

When I now look at the profile of the earlier days of my relationship with my partner, I see that many painful issues from my childhood were carried into the relationship (but not to the same intense extent) and, also, that I had married a woman who emotionally resembled my mother in terms of needs and the conditional giving of love. These issues did threaten our relationship but we were able to recognise them – me on my part and she on her part – and, with mutual support, move towards a more balanced, open, free and far less conditional type of relationship. I say 'far less conditional' because it takes considerable time and effort to reach the sublime heights of unconditionality but our aspirations sincerely lie in that direction.

Whilst I may have carried a protective self-image and ideal self into my marriage relationship, there were aspects of myself (and of my partner) that were not protective in nature and provided me with stepping stones to greater maturity. Certainly, my search for answers to my own misery, my ability to apply myself and my willingness to take academic and career risks helped me enormously. My childhood had also provided me with great self-reliant resources and these stood me in good stead during dark days of depression, loneliness and fear. In order to keep perspective, another wise question to ask regarding how you see yourself is: what character-istics do you possess that you can employ in your quest for greater personal maturity and a more fulfilling couple relationship?

CHANGING MY PROTECTIVE IMAGES OF SELF

I believe we all have a deep sense of our own goodness, unique-ness, wonder and vast potential but that we live in family, couple, community, school and political cultures that have made it unsafe to be open in such self-expression. We have all learned the hard lesson of repressing and suppressing the wonder of our unique beings in order to gain acceptance and recognition. We have necessarily and creatively allowed ourselves to follow values, ways, relationships and expectations that are artificial and conditional and that promote dependence and fear. To go against demands would mean risking the most devastating experience for the human psyche which is the withdrawal of love. As a child, you were ingenious in the means you developed to protect yourself from hurt. As an adult you can begin to free yourself of the shackles of artificiality, dependence, fear, hopelessness and depression. In order to do this, you must create an environment in which it is safe to be yourself, to be different, to express your uniqueness, to show unconditional regard for yourself, to state values that are caring of self, others and the world, and to be non-conformist. A tall order but one which you have all the power to achieve.

When you discover what led you to develop a protective self-image you have the answer to how to begin to move towards what I define as an open sense of self. When you are compelled to protect yourself, you close the doors on the wonder and potential of your own being. Developing an open feeling for self is reopening those doors and letting the light of your innermost goodness, worth and capability shine out into the world. You do not create your goodness or worth – it is a given. You cannot earn your sense of self through what you do. As you have seen, your goodness and worth are integral to your unique humanity, whereas self-image and ideal self have to do with behaviours. You are not your behaviour. Your behaviour is a means of experiencing yourself, others and the world. It does not add one jot to your value as a human being. That is not to say that your behaviours, accomplishments, knowledge, skills, artistry, creativity and so on are not praiseworthy, fascinating, interesting and credible. But the behaviour that is there today is gone tomorrow. Does that mean your sense of worth disappears too? You need to love and celebrate your own unique, wonderful being and not in any way tarnish that love by linking certain behaviours with your sense of self. A good relationship with self is a combination of loving yourself and deciding how you want to behaviourally be in this world.

So if actions add nothing to your sense of self, how then do you learn to appreciate self? From the moment of birth you are a unique phenomenon in this universe that will never be repeated. You are perfect in your being, a one-off happening. Your capability is limitless. Your sense of self is like the sun and just as the sun is always there but can be blotted out by black clouds, so too you are always of worth. Regrettably, this sense of self is clouded out in childhood years by the formation of a self-image and an idealised self. It is time to appreciate the cleverness of your self-image and ideal self strategies but to begin to let go of them as indicators of your worth. Recall that your self-image and ideal self have to do with behavioural judgments and expectations of you – they say absolutely nothing about your wondrous person. Enjoy your ways of living in this world but, most of all, see and hold onto your sense of self as being totally independent of anything you do or achieve.

The key means to rediscovering your self-worth is the creation of an intense, enduring, loving, accepting and affirming relationship with yourself. The causes of your loss of your sense of wonder of self were the early relationships between you and parents, teachers, siblings, adults and peers. The healing has to spring from the causes and consequently it is the establishing of an unconditional relationship with yourself that will gradually bring about your redemption of self. Your relationship with yourself needs to have all the characteristics that an unconditionally loving and affirming parent would bring to their relationship with their child. This relationship needs to be primarily emotional in nature so that all your thoughts and actions towards yourself are infused with a valuing and celebration of self. Love, acceptance and affirmation need to flow through all your daily experiences so that this tide of valuing actions sweeps away the old protective forces of self-image and ideal self.

Change comes about by ensuring that all actions are of a self-valuing and caring nature, whether they have to do with hygiene, rest, diet, physical exercise, work, leisure or lifestyle. Some examples are:

□ Value and unconditionally love yourself
□ Do things in a calm and relaxed way
□ Eat healthy foods
□ Give yourself adequate time to eat and digest

- ▢ Listen to yourself
- ▢ Encourage yourself to do your best
- ▢ View mistakes and failures as opportunities for learning
- ▢ Be assertive about your own beliefs and opinions
- ▢ Be spontaneous and open
- ▢ Be accepting of self
- ▢ Do not accept artificial goals that a partner or others may attempt to impose on you
- ▢ Be responsive to your own needs and to the reasonable needs of your partner or others
- ▢ Make time and space for yourself
- ▢ Take regular physical exercise
- ▢ Challenge yourself

Changing your protective images of yourself is an endless process that needs to be consistently worked on. The old protective ways are likely to be strongly ingrained and it is only through persistent practice of affirming and valuing actions that these old ways will be extinguished. The rewards of redeeming your unique sense of self are high: security, independence, freedom to be yourself, spontaneity, openness, rewarding intimate relationships, peacefulness and increased potential for self-fulfilment.

CHAPTER 5

HOW MY PARTNER SEES ME

To thine own self be true.
Shakespeare

Like you, your partner comes into the relationship carrying his personal emotional baggage and it is likely that both he and you will endeavour to establish distinct identities at the expense of each other's individual progress in life. The relationship will also suffer because of the unhealthy intertwining of intimacy and personal identity issues. Your partner may see you in ways that do not fit you, but when you are vulnerable, you are subconsciously compelled to protect yourself from his projections and you may find that you may have to suspend your own identity formation. This would be unfortunate because the welfare of a couple relationship depends critically on each person holding onto their own unique and distinct identity.

SELF AND IDENTITY

Two important issues in your relationship with your partner are developing your sense of self and continuing to fashion your own distinct identity. When you possess a strong sense of self, the process of identity formation is not paved with too many difficulties. However, when the contrary is the case (and this is more common) then considerable confusion and hardship attend your efforts at deciding who you are and how you want to be in this world. Much of your search for an identity is done during your adolescent years but, regrettably, many individuals do not reach any firm conclusions regarding themselves during these teenage years and, consequently, carry their unresolved identity issues into their adult life and into intimate and other relationships.

Depending on family dynamics, identity issues may be resolved in one of several ways. After a period of experimentation across a wide breadth of social, intellectual, sexual, philosophical, political, religious, spiritual and other dimensions, some young adults do come to a working definition of who they are and what directions they wish to further explore in life. Generally speaking, these adolescents would have had the benefit of a relatively secure upbringing where they felt loved largely for themselves and were given the freedom to responsibly explore the complex world of people and things. Unfortunately, most adolescents go through a prolonged state of identity confusion and emerge into adulthood with a poor sense of self and a weak individuality. In general they are highly dependent on the judgments and opinions of others, are indecisive, lack direction, hop from one experience to another but never attain mastery, are critical, blaming, passive or aggressive, and are slow to take responsibility for their own lives. The frequency, intensity and duration of these reactions to life will depend on the level of confusion and insecurity. Generally, after much soul-searching, and personal and interpersonal trauma, some level of personal identity emerges but this might not happen until quite late on in life. However, there are those adolescents who have experienced severe neglect during childhood and who suffer profound identity confusion; unless they get professional help, they are unlikely to ever arrive at a celebration and acceptance of self and a solid level of individuality.

Some young people develop what has been termed a 'crystallised' identity. These do not go through any experimentation phase nor do they experience any identity confusion. Nonetheless, they are highly immature because they blindly take on the characteristics, attitudes, philosophy, religion and often career choices of their parents. Difference was not tolerated in their families. These young people lack a distinct identity and tend to be conformist, rigid, perfectionist, inflexible, judgmental, fearful, insecure, high achievers, overambitious and dependent on academic and/or work performance. They do not question issues and are not analytical.

It is on the sandy foundations of moderate or profound identity confusion or crystallisation that many relationships falter.

A clear distinction needs to be made between a sense of self and identity. A sense of self has got absolutely nothing to do with the wide repertoire of knowledge, skills, experiences, attitudes and beliefs you have built up during your life. Neither is it connected to education, career or position in life. As already pointed out in Chapter 4, your sense of self is immutable, unique – in many ways indefinable.

The bedrock of identity formation is your sense of self. Identity can be defined as your sense of self plus your evaluation of what you perceive yourself to be in terms of what you have learnt to date. This latter learning is the product of your biographical history but also includes what you like and do not like about your behavioural repertoire. Another way of putting it is that identity is your sense of your unique and vastly capable self plus the sum of all your experiences to date. When you have a healthy identity, then you will see your worth as being independent of all behaviour, but you will add the dimensions of, say, kindly, optimistic, generous, loving, ambitious, artistic, creative as being part of your identity. When your definition of yourself is non-existent, blurred, vague and tentative, then you do not see your wondrous worth and neither do you have any clear definition of your achievements to date. You may consequently experience continuous personal and interpersonal upheavals during your life. When your identity is well formed, on the other hand, you will experience life and relationships as continuous challenges to be embraced and cherished.

Identity formation is an endless process. However, for your individuality to continue to expand throughout life, it is essential that when opportunities for change and development arise you have a clear picture of who you are and what you have achieved; this serves as the rung on the ladder for the ascent to a wider definition of yourself.

INTIMACY AND IDENTITY

Intimacy and identity may be strongly intertwined. It is as if a person comes into a relationship in search of the answer to the question 'who am I?' When partners can be supportive and understanding of the process of identity formation, then mutual individual growth will occur, leading to enhancement of the couple relationship. However, such maturity is rare and it is more common for the couple relationship to quickly come under strain from the demands of each partner's identity issues. When identity questions dominate the individual partners, differences between them become a threat to the task of establishing a sense of self. Indeed, their differences can become the battleground on which each tries to establish their own identity at the expense of the other. For example, partners who tend to dominate will push that their needs, careers and opinions are more important than those of their companions. On the other hand, partners who are eager to please in order to gain acceptance will suspend establishing their own distinct identity. The poorer the sense of identity of the individual partners, the greater the strain on the couple relationship.

There is a great difference between the couple relationship which is a supportive forum for identity formation and the couple relationship which blocks the creation of a distinct sense of self. In the former, the partners can accept that there are times when the other may not be in a position to respond to their needs for affirmation, acceptance, praise and recognition for accomplishments. In the latter, the absence of such responses can lead to hurt, anger, withdrawal, manipulation or aggression. It is not that breakdown of communication never occurs when partners are supportive of each other's individual growth process, but that when it does, the breach in the relationship is normally healed within a short time. A strong index of a healthy couple relationship is where each apologises regularly for any hurts caused. It is important that such apologies are sincere and that active efforts are made not to repeat the hurtful responses. On the other hand, a significant index of a dependent relationship is where both partners rarely if ever apologise.

Of course the ideal situation is where each partner comes into the couple relationship with a strong feeling of worth and regard for self and a clear-cut identity. Once that is present, regard for the partner will flow automatically. Furthermore, partners with a sense of worthiness and individuality will brook no disrespect or disregard from their companions but they will communicate any dissatisfaction in a way that does not undermine the other's sense of self. The partners who are secure will be concerned to create an environment that promotes the growth of self and partner and the couple relationship.

HOW MY PARTNER SEES ME AND HOW I RESPOND

Your partner may judge you to be timid, shy, reckless, aggressive, insensitive and so on; at the same time he may have certain expectations of you to be always there, to never say 'no' to requests made of you, to be successful, to be attentive, to be devoted only to him, to be in agreement with his views, ways, tastes, philosophy, religion and so on. These judgments and expectations may mirror your parents' typical interactions with you. If you have not freed yourself of your parents' narrow behavioural definitions and unrealistic demands of you by the time you have entered a couple relationship, then your partner's evaluations and expectations may reinforce the poor self-image and ideal notions of self you carry from childhood. Your partner now becomes the vulnerable parents who did not provide the safe climate for you to realise your good-ness, worth, value, potential and uniqueness. Just as you learned in childhood to protect yourself from the hurts of conditional loving by taking on your parents' projections and forming a self-image and ideal self in keeping with these definitions and demands, you now do likewise with your partner. To do otherwise would mean risking rejection, and you do not yet feel secure enough to take on such a traumatic experience. This reaction is an unwitting collusion with your partner's vulnerability and protective strategies, leading to a blocking of the mature development of you and your partner as individuals and a serious blow to the success of the couple relationship.

When the gap is wide between the judgments (for example, 'you're a fool', 'you're selfish') and the demands (for example, 'be successful', 'take care of me') made of you by your partner, then great stress and consternation can abide as you must put con-siderable strain on yourself to live up to the expectations. The strain on intimacy is also high. When the gap is narrow – for example, 'you're very capable' (self-image message) and 'look after me' (ideal self message) – then you feel confident in measuring up to the expectation. However, there is a vulnerability here also, since any evidence of not being able to cope or fulfil the needs expressed may lead to withdrawal of love. This couple relationship exists on the rocky ground of conditionality.

Many examples of such double-level messages exist in troubled couple relationships and these mirror the healing work that each partner needs to do so that their relationship will not perish on the rock of their personal insecurities.

SELF–IMAGE MESSAGE	IDEAL SELF MESSAGE
□ 'You're always complaining.'	□ 'Speak up for yourself.'
□ 'You're so insensitive.'	□ 'Be kind and caring.'
□ 'You think you know everything.'	□ 'You have to make all the decisions.'
□ 'You're always out.'	□ 'Don't leave me.'
□ 'You're so thick-headed.'	□ 'It's your job to look after our finances.'
□ 'You're weak when you become emotional.'	□ 'Be strong.'
□ 'You're frigid.'	□ 'Be sexy.'

When a couple send contradictory messages to each other, they not only block their individual development but also seriously hamper the growth of their relationship. It is not safe to be with one another when this kind of confusing communication is operating. If, for example, you send the message 'Don't upset me. Be open with me' you are attempting to protect yourself by preventing your partner from raising certain issues that threaten you and at the same time you are fearful of not knowing what might be going on in his life and so demand complete openness. This is a 'no-win' situation. Your partner now has to find ways to protect himself from rejection and may learn simply and cleverly to sidestep issues that lead to emotional histrionics and be open on issues that do not threaten you. Many needs and issues are then sent underground and the seeds of discontent are sown. It is important to see that when individuals bring vulnerability into a couple relationship, the double-level messages that affect self-image and ideal self, and the responses to them, are all attempts to reduce the possibilities of hurt and rejection. However, once protection is operating, growth in the areas of protection is suspended. For example, when there is a taboo on the expression of love feelings no growth can occur in that emotional aspect of the relationship.

The typical protective strategies that may operate in a relationship where intimacy and identity issues are protectively intertwined are: avoidance, hostility, compensation and, sadly, sometimes apathy.

Avoidant responses

Avoidance is the most common protective strategy in an insecure relationship. The examples below show how avoidance cleverly protects through not engaging in actions that threaten your sense of identity.

PROTECTIVE STRATEGY	PROTECTIVE MESSAGE
☐ Being frequently out of the home	☐ 'When I'm absent, I can't get hurt.'
☐ Being indecisive	☐ 'If I allow you to make all the decisions, then I can't be open to ridicule.'
☐ Being passive	☐ 'If I allow you to be in control, you have no grounds for criticising me.'
☐ Sulking and freezing when partner attempts to approach you	☐ 'If I make no approach and force you to approach me, then I can't be rejected.'

$\longrightarrow$

PROTECTIVE STRATEGY (cont.)	PROTECTIVE MESSAGE (cont.)
☐ Being silent	☐ 'If I say nothing, I can't be hurt by you.'
☐ Having no ambition	☐ 'If I don't take any risks, I can't fail you.'
☐ Using drugs or alcohol	☐ 'When I'm out of this world, I can't be hurt.'
☐ Withdrawing through apathy and depression	☐ 'If I'm so helpless, you can't expect anything of me.'
☐ Withdrawing by means of physical illness	☐ 'If I'm sick and not able to cope, then you will have to stop making excessive demands of me.'
☐ Withdrawing into fantasy, delusions and hallucinations	☐ 'It is not safe to be with you in the real world.'

Hostile responses

Next to avoidance, hostility, rebelliousness and aggression are the most common responses used by partners in an unfulfilling relationship. Because of stereotyping, men are more likely than women to employ aggression as a means of protection against actions and words that threaten their ways of seeing themselves. The protective ploy in the use of hostility is the controlling of your partner's responses to you.

PROTECTIVE STRATEGY	PROTECTIVE MESSAGE
☐ Being cross, unreasonable and irritable	☐ 'When I control you, you can't make demands that threaten me.'
☐ Engaging in tirades of abuse, name-calling and bringing up old hurts	☐ 'If I stop you from talking, then you can't say anything that threatens me.'
☐ Frequently arguing and fighting with your partner	☐ 'When I stop you from opposing me, then you can't threaten me.'
☐ Constantly contradicting anything your partner says	☐ 'So long as you're wrong and I'm right, I'm safe.'
☐ Threatening to leave the relationship, return to your home of origin or go off with somebody else	☐ 'When I threaten you into submission, then you can't leave me.'
☐ Forcing sexual intimacy	☐ 'When I force you to be sexually intimate, then I can't be sexually rejected by you.'

Compensatory responses

Compensation is an ingenious means of protection against failure and rejection. It is commonly employed in the kind of culture where success is a measure of a person's worth. In a couple relationship where one partner sets high ideals for the other, then compensation can become a weapon to protect against rejection. Its protection lies in the extremes to which a partner will go in order to please and measure up to the other partner's unrealistic expectations, thereby offsetting failure, criticism, hurt and withdrawal of love.

PROTECTIVE STRATEGY	PROTECTIVE MESSAGE
☐ Constantly overpleasing partner	☐ 'If I please you all the time, then I can never be hurt by you.'
☐ Agreeing with what your partner says and does	☐ 'If I agree with everything you say and do, then there is no reason for you to reject me.'
☐ Being the 'martyr' who carries all the responsibility of maintaining the relationship	☐ 'If I carry all the responsibility, then there is no reason for you to criticise me.'
☐ Overworking to earn enough money to meet all the demands of your partner	☐ 'If I give you everything you need, then you'll never have any cause to leave me.'
☐ Always having the home spotless and yourself immaculately groomed	☐ 'When everything is perfect for you, then you can never find any fault in me.'

Apathetic responses

Apathetic reactions occur in the situation where no matter what you say or do, you cannot impress the other person. This is an utterly pessimistic, hopeless and despairing relationship in which to find yourself. The consequences are extreme neglect of self and loss of interest in your partner and the couple relationship.

The hidden protective messages reveal the real purpose of these strategies. However, because the real messages are unspoken and because partners tend to protectively react to the overt verbal message, the problems in the relationship cannot be resolved by these strategies. The partner on the receiving end is likely to see the other's avoidance, hostility and apathy as rejection, and compensation as suffocation. Either way, the partner is likely to react by also using one or a combination of the protective strategies of avoidance, hostility, compensation and apathy. There now is a vicious cycle of protective responses between the partners and no mature movement can occur in this relationship. Because the relationship is not unconditionally loving and is not emotionally supportive, and because the limiting protective interactions continue, the self-image and ideal self of each partner are being continually adversely affected, individuality and identity formation are blocked and neither partner can achieve a real sense of self.

PROTECTIVE STRATEGY	PROTECTIVE MESSAGE
☐ Total withdrawal into inactivity and irresponsibility	☐ 'When I do nothing, then nothing can happen to hurt me.'
☐ Frequently 'taking to the bed' or showing feelings of deep depression, hopelessness and suicide	☐ 'It is safer to show no hope of life around you.'
☐ Severe neglect of physical welfare (for example, overeating, undereating, excessive drinking, drug addiction)	☐ 'If I have no life, then you can't take anything from me.'
☐ Absolute denial that any problem exists in the marriage	☐ 'If there is no problem, then I don't have to face the possibility of losing you.'
☐ Serious suicide attempts	☐ 'If I am dead, you cannot hurt me any more.'

HOLDING ONTO MY OWN IDENTITY

One of the crucial tasks in a couple relationship is to be able to hold onto your own sense of self and identity in the face of your partner having a different idea of who you are and how you ought to be. Holding onto your identity means seeing that no matter what your partner thinks, says or does it is a message about him and not about you. If you hear the verbal message or see your companion's actions as being about you, then you are in danger of losing the solid ground of your own good sense of self. Because most of us have not yet developed a strong acceptance of self and we come into relationships with a fair share of doubts about ourselves, we do not have the inner security to stay separate from our partners' demands, judgments, criticisms and controlling actions. As you have seen, your partner may unwittingly project onto you unmet needs both from childhood and the present time and expect you to be the all-giving parents that his parents were unable to be because of their own vulnerabilities. The difficulty about such projection is that your partner has a set idea of how you ought to be and when you do not measure up, then withdrawal or aggression may well follow. Your partner is now operating within the 'child' protective mode, has subconsciously abrogated responsibility for self and will feel rejected when you do not respond to these unrealistic needs.

If you yourself are dependent on such a partner, the danger is you may slip into either the 'parent' role of taking on the projected responsibilities or the counter 'child' role of sulking, complaining, withdrawal, aggression, resentment and so on. When you take on the parenting role, which can be either appeasing or dominating in nature, you collude with your partner's poor sense of self, dependence and unrealistic expectations of you. Furthermore, you will be compelled to suspend your own personal development and, because you create a parent–child couple relationship, the seeds for a troubled relationship are sown. The development of an insecure couple relationship will be much more rapid when your responses to your partner are ones that create a child–child relationship. This is the situation of constant bickering, fighting and vying with each other.

The mature response to a partner who sees you in ways that are not fair, just and affirming of your right to define yourself is to assert what you feel is unrealistic, state what you feel is fair and make it kindly but abundantly clear that you are not taking on responsibility for his happiness. What you are willing to provide is love, support, understanding and compassion for your partner to take on the responsibility for his healing of hurts from the past and growing in the present. You cannot afford to suspend, postpone or dilute your own personal journey of self-discovery because in doing that you yourself will overburden the couple relationship and put its continuing existence in jeopardy.

Projection onto each other can start very early in a relationship. I recall one man telling me that on his honeymoon his wife stormed, raged, went on a wild spending spree and refused to talk to him for the rest of their honeymoon because he had met some friends and arranged, with her agreement, to meet them for a game of golf one afternoon. Unfortunately, because he was a man who (protectively) hated conflict, he tried all sorts of ways to make it up to her and he dared not make any further such excursions. Fifteen years later, when he came for help, he was still allowing her to dominate him. Even reasonable social arrangements were met with controlling reactions on her part. He eventually managed to separate out from this relationship and began to find a sense of his own worth apart from his wife and family of origin. Later on he also entered a more fulfilling and equal relationship with another woman.

MEANS OF HOLDING ONTO YOUR IDENTITY

☐ Own all your behaviours as being a communication about you and not your partner

☐ Do not tolerate any behaviours either from yourself or from your partner that lessen your sense of self and distinct identity

☐ Affirm frequently your own uniqueness, vast potential, goodness and worth

☐ Affirm frequently your partner's uniqueness, vast potential, goodness and worth

☐ Identify and be strongly respectful of the personal characteristics, attitudes, feelings, skills, knowledge, philosophy and spirituality that are important aspects of your definition of yourself and your partner's definition of himself

☐ Take responsibility for your own identity formation

☐ Do not take responsibility for how your partner sees himself

☐ Create a supportive and caring environment for your partner's journey of self-discovery and request a similar milieu for yourself

Whilst the essential aspect of holding onto your own identity is the recognition that all behaviours coming from your partner are about him, there are other means that will help you in this process; these are set out below.

The owning of all your behaviours as being about you (and not about your partner) is as important as seeing your partner's behaviours as being about him. It is the reverse side of the same coin. Many people struggle with this concept of behaviour being always a communication about the source from which it emerges. Realising the logic of this perception provides you with considerable power, understanding, objectivity and compassion. For example, if you greet your partner with 'you're always late', it seems as if your message is about his lateness. However, when you own the message as being about you, you see it has to do with your need for your partner to be on time. A more accurate message would be 'I'm disappointed you're late and would like you to be on time in future.' A more extreme example would be where your partner has been verbally abusive or physically violent and you attack back with 'you bastard'. If you truly valued yourself, you would let your partner know in no uncertain terms that 'I deserve to be respected and valued in this relationship and if such behaviours are not forthcoming, I intend to take actions to ensure my safety in this relationship.' The 'you bastard' message fails to communicate any of the message you need your partner to hear. It is important to remember that you need to follow through in action what you say in words to demonstrate to yourself and your partner your respect for your own identity.

Tolerance of any behaviours on your part that are neglectful of yourself demonstrates a disrespect for self and poor identity formation; it also invites similar neglectful behaviour from others. Equally, being passive in the face of abusive behaviours coming from your partner shows a poor sense of self and weakness in individuality. It is important that judgments, unfair criticism, harshness, verbal or physical abuse, tirades, cynicism, sarcasm and comparisons with others – whether they come from yourself about you or from your partner about you – are not endorsed, but are quite soundly countered by a demand for caring responses.

Affirmation of your own uniqueness, goodness and worth is a means of being visible to yourself and makes it more likely that you will hold onto your sense of self in the face of 'neglectful' actions on the part of your partner. Your relationship with yourself is more important than that with your partner and yet it is the relationship that is most neglected in our culture. It provides you with the immense strength to maintain your wonderful presence in an intimate relationship. It also means that the relationship is not burdened by any dependence on your part.

An equally powerful strategy for holding onto your own identity is affirming your partner's uniqueness, capability, lovability and worth. This is the *sine qua non* of an intimate relationship and a further bonus is the well-documented fact that what you send out from yourself in a relationship is what you are most likely to get back.

Being aware and expressive of the aspects of your behaviours that are important to your definition of yourself is another key aspect of identity formation. It is equally important that you respect and value your partner's definition of himself. When your definition of your partner is contrary to how he sees himself, it is inevitable that conflict will arise, and vice versa. There is an implicit rejection when you want your partner to be other than how he sees himself to be, and when your partner is vulnerable, he will be sensitive and reactive to that rejection.

The responsibility for your identity formation lies with yourself and the same holds true for your partner. The notion that 'it is up to you to make me happy and feel good about myself' is a tremendous burden to place on the shoulders of your partner and does not bode well for the security of the couple relationship. Ironically, until you come to a place of acceptance of yourself and a clear sense of who you are and what you want to do with your life, all efforts on your companion's part to assure you of your uniqueness, lovability and capability, and to praise your skills, knowledge and opinions, will fall on deaf ears. Adults begin to be able to internalise affirmation and praise only when they can affirm and praise themselves. I have worked with many individuals who were surrounded by people who sincerely loved them but the walls of protective self-rejection kept out all of these messages.

Only when these people began to experience some love of self was it possible for them to receive love from others. Individuals in couple relationships need to take on the responsibility for loving self and forming a distinct identity; to forgo that responsibility means dooming yourself and the relationship to a dark and unfulfilling life. Indeed it is important that partners are assertive with each other on this basic responsibility. It certainly helps enormously when each provides for the other a supportive, compassionate, understanding and encouraging environment for this personal journey. Listening is far more important than talking when you are attempting to create for each other the safety for personal change to occur.

Holding onto your own identity, and affirming and encouraging the same process in your partner, will go a long way to ensuring the growth of the couple relationship. Whether or not your partner affirms your identity formation, you must take total responsibility for it. If you give in to your partner's definitions of you and his telling you what you are and how you ought to be, then serious difficulties will ensue at both a personal and interpersonal level.

When you do not take responsibility for identity formation or hold onto your own identity in the relationship, you cannot then truly see the uniqueness and distinct identity of your partner. Rather, protectively you will want your partner to be everything you feel you are not and so you will end up seeing neither yourself nor your partner.

PART IV

MYSELF, MY PARTNER

We

When you need me
to be part
of you
no me
where's we?

When we need we
to be one
no me
no you
who's we?

When we need we
to be two
a me
a you
we're we

Tony Humphreys

CHAPTER 6

CHOOSING MY PARTNER

*Constant togetherness is fine – but only
for Siamese twins.*

Victoria Billings

COMING TOGETHER

A fascinating and tantalising interplay occurs when you become
attracted to someone:

- □ Flashes of eye contact
- □ Passing by where the person is sitting or standing
- □ Brushing against the person
- □ Making discreet enquiries ('who is he?', 'is he involved with
  someone?', 'where does he work?')
- □ Getting a friend to check out whether the attraction is reciprocal
- □ Setting up 'accidental' meetings
- □ Picking up the phone and then replacing it when it is answered

All these strategies show that even before you begin a relationship,
you are already in the business of being cautious and protective of
yourself.

What is it that stops you from acting directly and clearly on
your attraction? An approach such as 'I am attracted to you and
wonder are you available or interested in exploring this attraction
with me?' is a rare phenomenon indeed. What stops you from

being open about your attraction to another are your doubts about your own physical, intellectual or social self and the fear of rejection that comes from these uncertainties. Cleverly you send out tentative signals so that the person to whom you are attracted is not sure whether or not you are interested in him. He certainly cannot show any direct refusal which would be too threatening to your sense of self. However, if he responds to one or more of the protective strategies – for instance, returning your gaze, smiling at you or not pulling away from an 'accidental' touch – you may now take the initiative to express your attraction and ask for a meeting. If a liaison emerges, your uncertainty about yourself has not been healed and so necessarily you will intensify the protective interplay by engaging in some of the following behaviours:

- Constant attendance on the person
- Making frequent phone calls
- Having daily meetings
- Much hand-holding
- Making efforts to discover the person's likes and dislikes
- Giving gifts
- Springing 'surprises' on the person
- Rarely saying 'no' to demands
- Finding out the person's birthday
- Overpleasing
- Being overcautious about not saying the wrong thing
- Not expressing concern over significant differences between you

If the object of your affections goes along with this dance and, indeed, makes similar movements, then the liaison will move to a more intimate phase. However, if the two people begin to be out of step with one another, then there will be either an abrupt ending of contact or meetings will gradually fade out. Out-of-step protective messages may be:

□ Making excuses not to meet
□ Arriving late for dates
□ Not reciprocating gifts
□ Wanting to go home early
□ Making poor eye contact
□ Withdrawing from physical contact
□ Showing few or no expressions of enjoyment
□ Having an immobile facial expression
□ Having a stiff or laid back body posture
□ Frequently bringing a friend along
□ Not suggesting another date
□ Being easily irritated

When there is a certain degree of harmony and reciprocal movement, then it becomes safer to begin to reveal aspects of your life, aspirations and ambitions as well as deeper needs such as:

□ Need for some level of commitment
□ Need for an exclusive relationship
□ Need for communication on innermost needs and wishes
□ Need for the other person to reveal more of themselves
□ Need for partial or full sexual gratification
□ Need for sensitivity to your feelings
□ Need for more time alone together
□ Need to be introduced to friends

This movement towards a deeper expression of needs and feelings may unearth hidden vulnerabilities. It is at this point in the relationship that signs of differences that threaten, and accordingly deeper protective behaviours, may begin to emerge. There may be differences in food taste or in the use of leisure time; there may be opposing ideas and practices in philosophy, religion and spirituality; there may be differences in sense of humour. Protectors that may begin to become more obvious at this point include:

▫ Discomfort with physical closeness
▫ Guilt feelings around sexual contact
▫ Strong reticence about self-revelation
▫ Obvious difficulties in the expression of feelings
▫ Inability to cope when the other person is upset, frightened, insecure or angry
▫ Addiction to work
▫ Overreliance on family of origin
▫ Dependence on alcohol
▫ Lack of initiative
▫ Overattentiveness to companion's needs but rarely any statement of own needs
▫ Frequent rows

When the parties to this relationship are dependent and insecure, it is possible that a blind eye will be turned to the presence of these serious differences and protectors. I have known many couples whose relationship was formed in the hell of constant fighting, bickering, sulking, physical violence, sexual disharmony, neglect of each other and insensitivity, and yet they went on to marry each other. They protectively deluded themselves that 'things will change once we get married'. Unfortunately, the opposite is far more likely to be the case. If commitment to meeting each other's needs is not there before living together, how is it possible for an out-of-step couple to respond when even deeper commitment is required? It is the couple who have largely managed to stay in tune with each other who are far more ready to negotiate living together or being married. The needs that now emerge require greater time and dedication to the relationship and the letting go of many of the activities of being single. However, it is vital that the two people in the couple do not lose sight of their need to be independent of each other and that they continue to develop their own identity and individuality. A fine balance between time and resources for each other and time for self-development is required. The couple who are dependent on each other put far too much pressure on their couple relationship and switch off the light of their own precious individuality.

Couple needs that are important following the commitment to set up a home together include:

☐ Emotional need for love, affection, warmth, closeness, support, compassion, understanding, nurturance and humour
☐ Need for couple time, space and resources to develop their emotional and sexual relationship
☐ Need of each partner for own physical space and privacy to develop skills, hobbies, interests, study, career, friendships and leisure
☐ Couple needs for social outings, recreation, friendship with others, companionship, and sharing of experiences, expertise and knowledge
☐ Physical needs of both partners for health, fitness, comfort, safety, food and warmth
☐ Respect for religious and spiritual needs

Responsiveness to these needs is what makes a couple relationship. Whether the couple are in a secure enough position to do this will reveal itself quite quickly when they begin to live with each other, after the 'honeymoon'.

MY CHOICE OF PARTNER IS PERFECT FOR ME

People who are vulnerable and protected are attracted to those who are also vulnerable and protected. On the surface it may often seem that the saying 'opposites attract' is true. For example, the aggressive person chooses a partner who tends to be passive, and vice versa. Other examples of opposites attracting are possessiveness being paired with elusiveness, perfectionism with carelessness, extroversion with introversion, pleasing others with pleasing self. There is unconscious wisdom in the choice of a seeming opposite. Indeed there is a threefold purpose to such a choice. Firstly, in choosing a partner who is opposite to you in behaviour, you effectively protect yourself from having to engage in that behaviour and so you wisely offset failure and rejection. Secondly, when you gain some level of personal security you have the ideal model in your partner for the behaviour you have not dared practise yourself. Thirdly, you also have the opportunity to heal old hurts in the safety of the supportive relationship with your partner. For example, the person who is aggressive needs to develop some of the passivity of their partner, and vice versa. Likewise, the partner who is reserved, shy and quiet can learn much from an extrovert partner and vice versa.

As pointed out, there is a clever inbuilt protectiveness in choosing a person who operates in an opposite way to yourself. Say, for example, you are the aggressive partner in a couple relationship; your partner, who is passive, may allow you to take the lead in decision-making so that he cannot fail, be criticised or rejected. When confronted about his passivity, he may rationalise it: 'I can't open my mouth without you flying off the handle.' A second protector is now operating: with his passivity reinforced by your aggression, the risk that would be involved for him in expressing needs, feelings and opinions is ingeniously eliminated. Of course, there is also protection on your part. Aggression is a means of forcing another to be always there for you, to agree with you, to be the same as you; now you have found a means of protecting yourself from rejection by your partner. A further protective effect is that the passivity of your partner reinforces your aggression and provides you with the rationalisation for maintaining your aggressive way of being: 'Nothing would get done around here if I didn't shout about it.'

A frequently occurring relationship is where a man who is behaviourally aggressive, dominant, critical and controlling becomes involved with a woman who is behaviourally passive, eager to please, non-assertive and docile. In such a relationship the man may be repeating the emotional patterns of his father and may have married or be in a committed relationship with a woman who behaves like his mother. The female partner may be behaving emotionally like her own mother and may have become involved with a man who behaviourally and emotionally resembles her own father. Both parties in this new liaison have emerged from families of origin that were neglectful of their emotional welfare. It is very likely that they will repeat the unfulfilling relationships of their parents, but glorious opportunities for learning from each other and developing a mature and fulfilling relationship are also present. It may appear insane for the man to have chosen a woman like his mother who, after all, did not protect him against the wrath and abuse of an aggressive father, but there is a threefold purpose to this seeming madness:

- ☐ to face his father within himself
- ☐ to face his mother within his partner
- ☐ to change from protective to open patterns of relating to self and partner.

Likewise, this man's partner, who is likely to have become involved with someone emotionally resembling her father and who is herself like her own mother, is also faced with similar healing opportunities:

- ☐ to face her mother within herself
- ☐ to face her father within her partner
- ☐ to change from protective to open patterns of relating to self and partner.

The male partner's first healing task is to face his father within himself. He needs to stand back from his aggressive behaviours and ask 'why am I employing these same ways of relating to my partner as my father did in his relationship with me and my mother?' He needs to return to his childhood and witness again the effects of his father's aggression on himself and on his mother. He needs to feel and heal the hurt, humiliation, rejection, fear, anger, rage and helplessness that he experienced as a child so that he can become steadfast in his resolve not to expose his partner to such an unhappy relationship.

The man's second task, to face his mother within his partner, involves not colluding with her passivity and actively encouraging and supporting her to give full open voice to her feelings, needs and concerns. He needs to re-experience how when he was a child his mother's passivity reinforced his father's aggression and left him unprotected. He needs to feel the sense of abandonment and disappointment he experienced when his mother (to protect herself) turned a blind eye to her spouse's neglectful actions. He now has the opportunity to caringly and strongly assert his need for his partner to take responsibility for herself and not accept or in any way collude with his aggressive behaviour towards her.

The third task entails creating a relationship with self and partner that mirrors unconditional loving, acceptance, openness, fairness, tolerance of difference, support, listening, valuing, understanding, gentleness, positive firmness, responsibility for self, encouragement, affirmation, good humour and a joyful approach to living.

Likewise, the female partner who is passive, timid and fearful needs to ask herself: 'why am I as an adult repeating my mother's ways of relating to my father and me?' She too needs to return to her childhood and feel again the effects of her mother's passive behaviours on her relationship with her spouse and on her as a child. She needs to see how she as a small child would have felt insecure, helpless and let down by her mother. She needs to witness how her mother's passivity fed the fires of her father's aggression. Out of the reliving of these experiences she can heal herself. She can then determine to let go of her protective passive strategies so that she, as a partner, does not abandon herself to a repeat fate of being bullied and dominated or neglected because of passivity on her part. When she does this, she has truly faced her mother within herself.

Her second task is to face her father within her partner. Once again it becomes necessary for her to recall the effects of her father's aggression towards her mother both on their relationship and on herself. She needs to allow to surface all the feelings of rejection, fear, rage, sadness, humiliation and helplessness so that she can become determined not to live under such a shadow in her relationship with her partner. She now must strongly assert to the father within her partner her right to be respected, loved, cared for, understood and accepted. She needs to let her partner know, in no uncertain terms, that she does love him but will not accept or tolerate any abusive behaviours on his part towards her. She is now facing the father within her partner, doing what she was unable to do as a child and what her mother had not done for her. What wisdom in choosing a man who emotionally resembled her father!

Her third task is the same as that described for her male partner. Essentially it involves becoming the positive parent towards herself that she lacked in her childhood and creating an open relationship with her partner that does not repeat any of the protective patterns of the relationship between her parents.

There is a fourth task that may be required of both partners which is that they separate out from their own parents and ensure that they are not continuing to be dependent on them, or controlled or manipulated by them. Separating out from parents does not mean ceasing to love them, but it does mean actively letting them know that you are now an independent adult, responsible for your own values, career choices and life.

The wisdom of opposites attracting can again be seen in the example of the woman who is the 'carer' who becomes involved with a man who is the 'taker'. I recall the case of a woman who, as a child, protected herself from rejection and gained conditional acceptance by adopting a caring role within her family. Her mother was critical and overdemanding while her father was passive, quiet and pleasing of his wife for 'peace sake'. The reinforcement she got for her caring role was great: avoidance of her mother's criticism and some recognition from her, and great praise and encouragement from her father, who used to call her his 'little mammy'. She used to cook the meals, clean the house, do the shopping, look after the laundry and take care of younger siblings. Not surprisingly, this early conditioning led her to take up the nursing profession and she also spent considerable time working in Third World countries. Wisely, as an adult she continued to gain acceptance and recognition from others through taking care of them.

People who are locked into a caring role maintain their protection at considerable physical, emotional and social costs to self; there is, however, an important gain which is the protection from criticism and rejection and the meriting of some form of recognition. It was quite a sad but freeing revelation for this woman when she had the safety to see that all her giving over the years to family and others had been driven by fear of rejection and the deep need to be loved and accepted. The giving was an unconsciously clever strategy to gain recognition. Before and for some time after she had arrived at the understanding of her drive to please, she had tremendous difficulty in saying 'no' to the demands of others. Ten years into her marriage she was sent to me suffering from ME.

Carers are people who exhaust themselves for others. As I probed into this woman's daily pattern of living and her experiences in her family of origin, I unearthed considerable hostility towards her partner (and, later on, towards her mother and father). I asked her: 'what is it in you that is making you cross and irritable in your marriage relationship?' Her answer was clear: 'I give and give and give but he never sees my needs.' But her husband was not responsible for her needs and neither could he read her mind. It was her responsibility to let him know clearly what her emotional, social, sexual, career, domestic, recreational and other needs were. In fact, her husband was the perfect partner for her and someone from whom she had much to learn (and vice versa). Unlike her, and like her own mother, he was an expert at identifying his own needs and demanding that they be met. He had come from a family in which he had been thoroughly 'spoilt'.

Children who are spoiled are used to getting their own needs met by others and this expectation continues into adulthood. However, such people are not good at taking responsibility for themselves. Children who are overindulged are disabled and emerge into adulthood being heavily reliant on others to meet their needs. When their demands are not responded to, they can be critical, sarcastic and aggressive. This woman's husband had unconsciously chosen her in order to continue the childhood pattern of being 'mammied'. But he also had the opportunity of learning from his wife that other people have needs as well.

When they both discovered the sources of their personal and marital difficulties and both made genuine efforts to move away from the protective patterns of behaviour learned in childhood, their relationship matured and deepened. A relationship can be a tremendous source of safety, support and encouragement to be yourself and to be open with each other. The woman's task was to establish an identity distinct from the role of carer, to begin to assert her own needs within the relationship and to become independent of her partner. Her husband's task was to establish his identity distinct from being the 'spoilt boy', to learn to recognise and to respond to the needs of his wife as well as of himself and to stand on his own two very capable feet. Communication in their relationship became much more direct and clear. Both of them learned to recognise and take responsibility for their own needs and to express them within the relationship without expectation that they have to be met.

If 'opposites attract', as often seems to be the case, it is equally true to say that 'birds of a feather flock together'. But the similarity is at the deeper level of personal vulnerabilities and childhood experiences of hurt, humiliation, physical, emotional or sexual abuse, unfair expectations, conditionality and, sometimes, outright abandonment. In this case, the woman and her husband were opposites in the way they got their needs in life met, but were similar in that they were both highly dependent because of their conditional upbringing. The condition for love for her was 'be the carer' and for him 'be helpless'. Each of them emerged from their families of origin with unresolved issues with both their parents and considerable personal vulnerability. This then was the emotional baggage that brought their relationship to crisis point where the opportunities for change were enormous.

The paradox of opposites attracting and underlying similarities being present at the same time in a distressed relationship demonstrates the subtle and creative complexity of human relationships. The opposing behaviours that a couple bring to a relationship offer the behavioural means to each other (when each is emotionally ready for change) to tackle and heal the unresolved childhood conflicts. It is at this deeper level that there is strong similarity between the partners and hence it can be said that problems marry problems: individuals with a poor sense of self become involved with people with a similarly low sense of self, and people with poor identity formation are attracted to those whose individuality is similarly blurred or unformed. The attraction of sameness also offers a powerful protection because you are more likely to feel attracted to someone like yourself; you certainly would feel extremely threatened by an approach from somebody who is very secure and sure of self. The risk of 'not being good enough' is too great and you will seek the shelter of your own kind until you have achieved some sense of your own goodness and worth.

THE IDEAL CHOICE OF PARTNER

Hindsight is a great educator. A frequent cant in troubled couple relationships is 'if I knew then what I know now, I would never have become involved with someone like you', or 'if I had known that this is what marriage is like, I would have stayed single', or 'I should have known better than to marry you'. To employ hindsight as a stick to beat either yourself or your partner is a protective ploy that postpones or distracts from the actions that are needed to break the cycle of unhappiness in the couple relationship. If you want to be wise after the fact, then focus on the changes that are needed here and now to heal whatever personal and interpersonal issues are causing disharmony between you and your partner. Of course, it would prevent a considerable amount of emotional pain if prospective partners had some awareness of the characteristics to look for in each other that go some way towards ensuring the emergence of a mature and loving couple relationship. Some of the characteristics of those ready for a mature and harmonious relationship are given below. Few of us are in a position to be that clear in choosing a partner because our choice of partner is often guided by unresolved childhood conflicts. However, there will be individuals who are in a position to hear and follow the guidelines below, and there will come a time when other couples will be ready to take on the necessary actions that bring about couple harmony.

If prospective partners or, indeed, partners within an already established couple relationship fail to meet any one of these guidelines, it is important that they set about improving the particular areas where there is a shortfall. Awareness of what is required may not necessarily lead to the working commitment needed to achieve these desirable goals. In addition to awareness, there needs to be emotional security. The primary emotional security is within each individual partner and as such acts as a basis that typically leads to a determination to fulfil oneself at both personal and interpersonal levels. When interpersonal security and safety exist, whereby both partners feel assured of love and respect in spite of differences and difficulties, then progress towards attaining these goals is considerably easier.

THE IDEAL PARTNER

- ☐ A strong sense of one's own worth and value as a unique person
- ☐ Ability to unconditionally love, value, respect and honour one's partner
- ☐ Ability to live in the here and now
- ☐ Ability to communicate directly and clearly
- ☐ Ability to express and respond to feelings in oneself and in one's partner
- ☐ Ability to be responsible for the control of one's own behaviours and to expect similar responsibility on one's partner's part
- ☐ Ability to support and enhance one's partner's sense of worthiness, value and uniqueness
- ☐ Ability to withstand, cope with and resolve the inevitable relationship pressures and stresses that arise
- ☐ Ability to respect, value and meet the reasonable emotional, social, educational, creative, spiritual, physical, behavioural and independence needs of oneself and one's partner
- ☐ Ability to express, enjoy and respond to the sexual needs of oneself and one's partner
- ☐ Ability to appreciate and celebrate the differences between oneself and one's partner
- ☐ Ability to resolve family and couple difficulties that arise

Neither you nor your partner needs to have fully attained all these goals before making a commitment to one another; if that were the case, very few would form couple relationships. However, if there is a serious lack in relation to any one of the goals, this would need to be seriously considered before embarking on living together. Growth both at a personal level and at the relationship level would need to occur before a decision to live together is made. If the deficits are not too serious, then a determination on the part of both partners to caringly and firmly stay alert to and work on the issues will be sufficient to enable a real commitment to each other to be made. Indeed, it is the very admittance of vulnerability that makes personal and interpersonal growth likely to continue. Furthermore, mature partners know that rifts, vulnerabilities, differences, mistakes and failures are glorious opportunities for deepening their intimacy. If there is an issue of concern to you, do not wait for your partner to take the initiative on raising it. Take the lead yourself; when you do, you strengthen yourself enormously and you also provide the example and safety for your partner to begin also to take the initiative.

CHAPTER 7

LIVING WITH MY PARTNER

*People are lonely because they build walls
instead of bridges.*

Joseph Fort Newton

LIVING WITH THE DIFFERENCES BETWEEN US

Individuals bring their vulnerabilities and unresolved childhood issues into the couple relationship, and most of the interactions between them are affected by these doubts, fears and insecurities. It is known that the first two years of living together are the most trying, giving rise to the saying 'love is blind but marriage is an eye-opener'. However, the fact that you chose the perfect partner for you to heal and move on from your unresolved childhood conflicts makes nonsense of this saying. It is more accurate to say that 'love is all-seeing and living together is a cure for past blindness'. The pressure in the early years of living together arises because the couple are attempting to accommodate each other's differences against the background of their individual insecurities. Of course, the more opposite in ways that the couple are, the greater the level of difference.

Differences between a couple can be challenging and exciting and provide opportunities to learn from each other. However, when one or both partners are emotionally vulnerable, then differences are a major threat and can become the battleground or the silent-ground on which each partner struggles with identity questions. For example, partners who employ aggression as a protection against hurt and rejection will insist that their needs, career, opinions and so on are more important than those of the other person. On the other hand, partners who employ the protection of passivity will sacrifice their own individuality and independence for the sake of acceptance (limited though it may be) from the other and 'for peace sake'. The deeper the vulnerabilities of the partners, the longer the problems and conflicts will endure. No change will happen until a breakthrough occurs which will allow for the personal and interpersonal growth of each partner.

In the meantime the relationship will continue to be characterised by the protective patterns of relating that were there at the beginning of the relationship but had not yet posed a major threat to the emotional well-being of either partner and their relationship with each other. Once such threats occur, there will be an escalation of existing protective means of relating and even the creation of new protective strategies. Protectors are there to reduce possibilities of rejection; it is only when they begin to fail in this task that an escalation ensues. Sometimes a 'pseudo peace' can be established between a conflicting couple as a result of the emergence of new protectors or an increase in old ones which creates a new status quo. However, the hidden vulnerabilities and insecurities have not been resolved and it is likely that at some future point the underlying dissatisfactions will break through the facade of the protectors. This breakthrough would be a desirable happening but there are some couples whose level of personal and interpersonal unsafety is so great that they necessarily hide behind the protective (and always limiting) nature of their relationship for their lifetimes.

There are others where the escalation of protective forces leads to extremes of violence, shouting, neglect, sexual abuse, denigration of each other, unending hostile silences and so on. The possibility of safety ever being created within these couples is very low and an irretrievable breakdown in the relationship is likely. It is important that such individuals attempt to find safety outside the relationship in order to have the care and support to be able to extricate themselves from such an unhappy existence. If they do not find this support, conflicting couples can remain inextricably bound to each other for life.

WHEN TWO PROTECTIVE WORLDS COLLIDE

When old protective ways fail to ward off hurt in the partnership, new protectors are likely to emerge. The more typical protective strategies are:

- □ 'passing the buck' of responsibility (blaming of partner for how you feel)
- □ 'taking the buck' of responsibility (internalising blame by partner and blaming self for how you feel)
- □ distancing strategies
- □ binding strategies.

'Passing the buck' of responsibility

A major protective device in a troubled couple relationship is blaming your partner. Blaming is an attempt to put the spotlight and responsibility for how you feel and act onto your partner. This is immensely clever because it means you do not have to look at yourself or take on any responsibility for how you feel. Consequently you do not have to face your own vulnerabilities, the protective parent within yourself and the parent within your partner. It also means you do not have to take on the risk of engaging in any healing actions that could lead to failure on your part or rejection by your partner.

People who see their partners as responsible for their needs and welfare will employ a host of blaming strategies when needs are not met or when they feel anxious, lonely or depressed. Such blaming behaviours may be categorised as:

- aggressive 'passing the buck' strategies
- passive-manipulative 'passing the buck' strategies
- passive-aggressive 'passing the buck' strategies.

Aggressive strategies

Examples of aggressive 'passing the buck' strategies include:

- Blaming ('You made me angry.')
- Criticising ('Don't talk about things you know nothing about.')
- Controlling ('I don't want to hear you talking about any of your feminist ideas when we have company this evening.')
- Ridicule ('What would you know about anything?')
- Cynicism ('I wouldn't expect anything better from you.')
- Sarcasm ('You might as well be dead around here for all the attention you get.')

All these messages project your hidden needs onto your partner and are attempts to make your partner responsible for your needs. If the partner receiving these messages is equally vulnerable, he will not have sufficient emotional safety to read between the lines, and either will be busily defending self against the 'put down' behaviours or will withdraw emotionally and physically.

Possible hidden needs buried in the above projections are:

- 'When I come home and you barely greet me, I feel angry and I need closeness with you.'

- □ 'I feel embarrassed when you pretend knowledge of a subject and I would prefer you to honestly express your lack of knowledge in such a situation.'
- □ 'I feel excluded and sometimes put down when you voice your feminist ideas and I am requesting that you express your ideas in a way that doesn't do that to me.'
- □ 'I feel threatened when you show greater knowledge of a subject than I do and I feel embarrassed by my own lack of education.'
- □ 'I feel put down when you communicate sarcastically and I need you to express yourself more directly and respectfully.'
- □ 'I worry that I no longer matter to you.'

The sad thing is that when a relationship is under threat, it is unlikely that the real needs will be seen and a cycle of protective inventiveness will drive the couple further and further apart.

Aggressive 'passing the buck' protectors are easily detectable but though less visible both passive-manipulative and passive-aggressive strategies can equally drive a wedge between the couple.

Passive-manipulative and passive-aggressive strategies

Protective passive-manipulative and passive-aggressive strategies can be both verbal and non-verbal. Examples of non-verbal projections include:

- □ Physical withdrawal
- □ Emotional withdrawal
- □ Sulking
- □ Sexual withdrawal
- □ Addictive behaviours such as overdrinking, overeating, starving yourself, compulsive gambling, unprescribed use of tranquillisers

- Hurting yourself, for example pounding fist, foot or head off a solid object, or, more alarmingly, cutting yourself or drug overdosing
- Silence that may go on for weeks on end
- Damaging an item of value to your partner

Examples of verbal strategies are:

- 'You don't love me any more.'
- 'You wish I weren't here, don't you?'
- 'I'll just pack up and go.'
- 'Your work is more important to you than I am.'
- 'I'll never open my mouth again.'
- 'I'll go home to mother.'
- 'Isn't it better we part?'
- 'I know you wish you never got involved with me.'
- 'I'll just leave.'
- 'What's the use of talking?'

All these behaviours – both verbal and non-verbal – indirectly blame your partner and the implied message is 'look at what you are driving me to do'. Such protectors have the subconscious purpose of making your partner feel bad and guilty in the hidden hope that he will change in behaviour towards you. These projections involve no risk for the sender but they do involve risk for the receiver. If the receiving partner continues to pursue his right to act on certain needs – for example, to see some friends once weekly – he now risks coming home to a partner who is drunk or hostile, or who has taken a drug overdose or gone on a spending spree. The strategy is extremely clever; however if the receiving partner gives in to the manipulation then both partners' individual development is blocked, huge resentment will develop in the receiving   partner, and their relationship will remain insecure and troubled.

It is important to see how 'passing the buck' actually protects the sender of the message. If you say, for example, 'you make me mad', you load all the responsibility for your feelings onto your partner and take no emotional risk yourself in terms of failure, refusal or rejection. When you send a direct and open message such as 'I feel angry when you apparently don't listen to me and I believe I deserve the respect of being listened to', then the risk of ridicule or rejection is greater. If your partner is vulnerable, he may protectively respond to such an open message with 'what's there to listen to?', leaving you in an even more unsafe and distressed state. The important point here is that the person who sends a blaming or manipulative message is not consciously trying to hurt or put down the other partner, but is attempting subconsciously to prevent any possibility of hurt or rejection. Nevertheless this protective type of communication inevitably leads to distancing within the couple relationship, a lowering of interpersonal safety and a lowering of both partners' sense of themselves.

It can be a wonderful revelation for a couple to realise that no matter what one says to the other, it is always something about the sender even though it may appear to be about the receiver. For example, if you say to your partner 'you only think about yourself', you need to ask yourself 'what is my hidden need in that criticism?' The reply you give yourself may be 'he never thinks about my needs' (still blaming). Ask yourself another question, 'what are the needs I want him to notice?' Now the real issue is likely to emerge: 'well, I would like him to notice when I'm tired or when I'd like a break from the children or a night out with my friends or the encouragement to pursue my career'. This process has now led to a revelation of your own needs, a far cry from the original blaming message 'you only think about yourself'. Having identified your unmet needs, it is your responsibility to express them and to find fair ways to have them met.

'Taking the buck' of responsibility

Blaming self is apparent where the person's identity is protectively dependent on the opinions and reactions of others. 'Taking the buck' of responsibility occurs when the person receiving the message internalises the communication as being about self rather than being about the sender. When the message is critical or abusive, then the receiving partner will feel hurt, rejected and 'put down'. Likewise, the partner who internalises a compliment sees the other as having greater knowledge about the receiver than does the receiving partner. Many partners feel good about themselves only when they have been affirmed or complimented by their partners; they possess no sense of wonder or good about themselves and are left bereft when their partners fail to notice or provide feedback to them.

The person who protectively internalises what their partner says appears hypersensitive to criticism, easily hurt and vulnerable, and as someone in need of protection. This person's partner can respond to the need for protection by either pussyfooting around the person or avoiding any confrontation. The 'taking the buck' strategy is now effective in meeting the aim of reducing experiences of hurt and rejection. Nevertheless, protective reactions of one partner to the self-blaming of the other partner mean that communication between the couple is either vague or absent with a consequent build-up of a whole range of unspoken and unmet needs. At the point when unmet needs reach a peak level, the protective strategies of both partners will break down and a crisis will develop. At this point couples who are highly insecure may resort to more extreme protective strategies, for example sickness and violence. The couple where even one partner has some good sense of self is in a better position to avail of the opportunity present in the crisis for real and lasting emotional change.

Blaming self arises from protective dependence on the other for acceptance, approval, affection and caring, with consequent fears of rejection, criticism, disapproval and failure. Dependence, in turn, is a product of a protective poor view of self which itself originated in response to unfair demands and conditional or totally neglectful parenting. It is good to see this creative process clearly, as reducing or overcoming blaming your partner or blaming self is an integral part of the process of healing couple conflict. The illustration below shows that these processes are but the crest of a wave of an underlying sea of emotional distress.

BLAMING YOUR PARTNER OR SELF-BLAMING

Fears of hurt, rejection, failure, criticism

Dependence on partner for acceptance/approval

Middle/poor self-image and unrealistic ideal self

Unhealed childhood wounds
(due either to conditional or to emotionless
or very neglectful parenting)

It is not difficult to see how blaming others protects you from hurt, criticism and rejection, but self-blame too has a similar if less detectable purpose. For example, if your partner says to you 'you're stupid' and you personalise this by passively agreeing, the passive reception of the judgment protects you from any further criticism, ridicule, hurt or rejection. There is a further protective function to internalising the messages coming from your partner and that is that you do not have to face up to your own vulnerability and unhealed childhood wounds. Furthermore, in seeing yourself as 'stupid', 'slow', 'weak', 'unattractive', 'timid', 'fearful', 'shy' and so on, you cleverly reduce your partner's and other people's expectations of you.

Another type of self-blaming is where you subconsciously rationalise: 'If I become like my partner, then he will not leave or hurt me.' People who continually try to please their partners take on their ideas, values, characteristics, opinions, dress and tastes in order to be accepted and valued. More than likely, these partners who are pleasing and appeasing in behaviour are continuing the protectors that worked for them in childhood in relation to their fathers or mothers. These attempts in the present to please others reflect their own poor sense of self, their reliance on their companions for acceptance and love, and their need to protect themselves from any further experiences of emotional abandonment.

Sometimes, the person who internalises a criticism from a partner may project back onto the offending partner with an aggressive retort. For example, in response to the criticism 'you're stupid', the partner may retort, 'you're not exactly gifted with brains yourself'. This now smartly puts the spotlight back onto the partner who sent the critical message in the first place. Once the attention is off the initial receiver of the message, that person has managed to reduce the threat to sense of self.

A surprising revelation for the person who introjects is that anything anyone says is about the person who says it. If you receive your partner's message as being about you, then you have totally, but cleverly, misinterpreted the message; the focus goes on yourself and, whether you passively withdraw or aggressively attack back, you have not heard the need of the partner who sent you the message. Communication breaks down if sufficient interpersonal and personal safety is not present to enable each partner to stay separate and open to the other's messages. If you manage to stay separate from your partner's communication and try to discover what it is saying about him, then communication will stay open and positively flowing and the chances of your partner having his needs met are much greater.

An example will illustrate this process of letting go of protective self-blaming. Suppose your partner says to you 'you're so selfish'; rather than hearing the message as being about you, you hear it as being about the sender, and you want to discover the hidden issue behind this blaming message. You return the message to your partner by saying: 'In what way do you feel I'm selfish?' The answer you will get back will probably be another protective communication: 'You only think about yourself, never about me.' However, this retort is closer to the real need and you may now reply: 'In what way do I never think of you?' At this point it is likely that the full hidden issue will emerge: 'Well I feel you never ask me about how my day was or how I am feeling.' Now you can reply: 'I'm truly sorry that I haven't done this but I am happy that you are now revealing those needs to me and I will do my best to meet them.'

Blaming and self-blaming are best seen not as negative but as protective. Until a forum of personal and interpersonal safety is created to allow personal vulnerabilities to be healed and childhood relationship patterns to be explored and gently changed, the partners will continue to use such protective means of communication.

Distancing strategies as protectors

Distancing strategies serve the function of avoiding emotional or sexual intimacy where these are felt to threaten the security of the couple relationship and the sense of self of both partners. They signal deep levels of emotional unsafety and the need for considerable healing at both personal and interpersonal levels.

Distancing strategies may take the form of:

- Being busy
- Being absent
- Having 'no go' areas of conversation or action
- Involving a third party in the threatened relationship
- Having frequent disagreements over domestic affairs and responsibilities

In the 'being busy' pattern one or both of the partners employ work or some hobby or interest to fill all their time. Being busy is a cleverly designed subconscious strategy to avoid intimacy because the risk of conflict is perceived to be great when emotional closeness occurs. This protection may have been used by one of the partners' parents and is now unearthed in the repeat pattern of their son's or daughter's problematic couple relationship. In some families a display of spontaneous affection and warmth can be greeted with a dismissive remark: 'don't be silly', 'don't go all soft on me now', 'what's this nonsense all about?' The family member now learns to protect self by freezing love feelings. If, later on when an adult, the child of such a family becomes involved in a committed relationship with someone who is opposite and is emotionally gushing, the employment of a distancing strategy may become necessary when their partner begins to press hard for affection.

'Being absent' can take the form of being thoroughly absorbed in some leisure or work pursuit such as reading, watching television, gardening, fishing, car maintenance, house-cleaning, child-rearing and so on. The 'absent' person is not 'tuned in' to their partner's life as this might mean facing needs and issues that threaten the personal security of the 'absent' partner and the present status quo of the relationship. The 'being absent' protective strategy is frequently used in relationships where sexual intimacy threatens one or both partners. Both personal and interpersonal safety will be needed before a partner will be willing to let go of this strong strategy.

'No go' areas are commonly present in threatened couple relationships. The protection is obvious: if these 'no go' areas are not brought up for discussion or acted upon, then they pose no personal or couple threat. Deeper issues lie behind 'no go' areas and these bans will not be lifted until deep healing has occurred. Examples of 'no go' areas are:

- □ 'Don't talk about my family.'
- □ 'Don't mention intimacy.'
- □ 'Don't bring up the topic of sex.'
- □ 'Keep my mother out of the conversation.'
- □ 'Don't ask me about my work.'
- □ 'Don't request extra money.'
- □ 'Holidays abroad are out of the question.'
- □ 'Don't make any remark about my thinning hair.'
- □ 'Don't say anything about my weight.'
- □ 'I don't want to hear about your problems.'

These 'no go' topics are actually windows into the very areas in the individuals themselves and their relationship with each other that need to be tackled, but such openness and directness are not possible at this point because of the vulnerability of each of the partners.

Triangulation is a very common protective device that emerges in problematic couple relationships. Anything between 60 and 80 per cent of partners engage in a relationship outside their primary commitment. Triangulation refers to the situation where a third party is brought into the fray to serve the subconscious protective purpose of distracting the couple from their own conflict. A frequent example of triangulation is where one of the partners has an extra-relationship affair. For example, the female partner takes a lover in order to have emotional and other needs met, needs which are not being recognised by an emotionless or a 'too busy' partner. She is too vulnerable to make emotional demands on her male partner since the risk of ridicule, coldness and rejection is too high. It seems easier not to confront and thus, protectively, she becomes open to an extra-relationship affair. All appears well until the affair becomes known. Now the male partner will typically focus his attention on the lover but will not confront the real issue of the problematic relationship between him and his partner. Sometimes a male partner who is passive in behaviour may actually encourage the relationship as it means that the underlying conflict is totally avoided. In spite of the triangulation situation, neither partner may want to leave the other. The lover becomes 'pig in the middle' and may suffer at the hands of both these unhappy partners. Separation can sometimes occur if the lover pushes for a commitment but very often what results in this case may be described as 'going from the frying pan into the fire'. A successful relationship depends on the presence of emotional safety, the healing of old and new wounds (both personal and interpersonal), and at least the beginnings of unconditional relating. Such issues will not have been resolved if one partner jumps from one relationship into another – an all-too-frequent happening nowadays.

Another common distancing strategy in conflictual couple relationships is frequent petty quarrels over domestic issues such as who does the washing up, who cooks, who cleans the house, who washes the car, who does the ironing, who does the garden, whose night out is it and so on. Petty disputes serve the purpose of screening the couple from deeper emotional issues which need to be faced but which are too threatening to their individual sense of self and their relationship to be voiced.

It is vital to understand that the partners in a conflictual relationship do not set out deliberately to hurt each other, and their sometimes extreme behaviours are only attempts to allay their worst fears about themselves as individuals and the stability of their relationship. Where couples have not separated out from their families of origin and are still experiencing identity confusion, distancing strategies will be frequent, intense and often extreme.

Binding strategies as protectors

Binding strategies refer to protective attempts by people to tie their partners to them by:

□ Possessiveness
□ Martyrdom
□ Suicide threats
□ Suicide attempts
□ Threats
□ Manipulation
□ Sickness

The subconscious strategy here is to make it virtually impossible for your partner to be either out of sight or capable of managing without you.

The partner who employs the protector of possessiveness constantly clings, needs frequent reassurance, lives 'in the partner's pocket' and is easily upset when a need is not met. Frequently, this person's equally vulnerable partner will acquiesce to these unrelenting demands; they cannot do without a partner and even a suffocating relationship protects from having to face the lack of a separate identity and a high level of dependence. Thirteen per cent of widows and widowers die within six to twenty-four months of the death of their spouses. I have known people who died within weeks, days and even hours of their partner even though none of them showed any signs of illness at the time of their partner's death. It is as if when one partner dies the remaining partner has no sense of self or of life without the couple relationship. The enmeshment of identity with intimacy is very clear in such relationships. As long as the protective behaviour of possessiveness works, these partners will not face the vulnerable nature of their relationship and their own individual immaturity.

The 'martyrs' are the people who make themselves indispensable to their partners. This person does everything for the partner and is extremely threatened when the partner attempts to do anything for self. Again, the subtlety and wisdom of the strategy are commendable. Once you have made yourself indispensable, how could your loved one ever leave you? Partners who accept being looked after do so in order to protect themselves from having to take responsibility for themselves.

Manipulation is yet another means by which some people keep their partners tied to them. Sexual manipulation is common in problematic relationships where sexual activity becomes a weapon to be wielded in the face of any threat to self or the relationship. Other manipulative strategies include sulking, hostile silences, withdrawal, non-cooperation, spending sprees, overcontrol of finances, histrionic outbursts and suicide threats or attempts. All these manipulative strategies are directed at ensuring that your partner is always there for you so that you are protected from any feelings of hurt or humiliation and from any possibility of the partner leaving you. Deep down you do not feel good enough about yourself to feel that your partner really loves you.

Sickness can be an extreme form of manipulation. Here the person unconsciously develops an illness or incapacity in order to tie the partner totally to them and to avoid the risk of rejection that comes from being active in the relationship. I recall many cases of overburdened partners telling me how happy their partners were following an illness that left them house-bound and totally in need of care. Prior to their illnesses, these 'sick' partners were excessively threatened by any responsibility. They often had been 'spoilt' as children, and as adults in a couple relationship they continued the pattern of needing someone else to take responsibility for them. They could not live without their 'overcaring' partners, and sickness made sure of their partners being life-bound to them. Of course, there is a protective pay-off for those partners who collude with this helplessness: the fact that they are needed makes them feel secure that the relationship will not flounder. The cost is great to both partners in terms of their limited individual development and the impoverishment of their couple relationship.

CHAPTER 8

DEEPENING THE RELATIONSHIP

Let there be spaces in your togetherness.

Kahlil Gibran

EMOTIONAL SAFETY ENABLES GROWTH

Probably one of the strongest revelations within this book is that partners will protect themselves in multiple and ingenious ways from reliving old hurts or experiencing new ones. When there is protection, it means that sufficient emotional safety is not present in the relationship for one or both partners to be open on certain feelings, needs, wishes, desires, difficulties and aspirations that they need to voice. Somehow there is either a covert or overt message that you do not bring certain issues to light. Overt examples might be: 'don't mention my parents', 'I don't want to hear about you wanting to go out to work', 'don't mention our sexual difficulties', 'don't cry', 'don't show anger', 'don't be sick', 'don't mention money'. Covert bans are communicated non-verbally when any attempt is made to raise a taboo issue: stiffening of the body, becoming tight-lipped, emotional withdrawal, physical withdrawal, hostile silence, taking to the bed, getting up and walking out, a cross look, a thunderous facial expression, non-listening and changing the subject. Even though there is no verbal ban, you know full well danger lurks if you pursue your course. If you are insecure and dependent, you may well give in to the covert restrictions. This means that many of your needs go abegging and the beginnings of a tide of resentment and frustration will well up in you and probably lead to emotional withdrawal from your partner. No progress can now occur in this relationship because protective walls of fear, withdrawal, threat and hostility are being built up by both partners. There is some hope when one partner continues to kindly but firmly push against the castle walls. You cannot allow the protective barriers of your partner to block your own progress through life. However, to do that, you yourself require certainty of self. It is far easier when a climate of emotional safety exists between partners.

Emotional safety abides where there is an atmosphere of openness and affirmation, direct and clear communication, listening, acceptance of differences, negotiation on difficulties, and an assurance that no matter what you say, do, believe and aspire to you will not be judged or criticised by your partner. This does not mean that your partner has to agree with you at all times. On the contrary, you would want him to express his own needs, feelings, thoughts and ambitions but in a way that does not 'put down' your way of being. It is within this atmosphere of respect for each other's differences that true movement towards meeting each other's needs can be made. If you constantly tell your partner 'you're wrong and I'm right', then you do not make it safe for your partner to be himself and to be different from you. You are instead judging and making unrealistic demands (mostly, 'be like me') of your partner. Inequality, fear, injustice, dominance and judgment now mark this couple relationship. No person deserves to live within this autocratic regime.

The basis for creating the emotional safety for your partner to be himself is your own strong and sure sense of self (see Chapter 4). When you are self-possessed, you are not threatened by your partner's differences from you; on the contrary, you are challenged and educated by them. The steps involved in setting up emotional safety are:

- □ Continued work on the development of your own good sense of self
- □ Provision of affirmation and support for your partner's development of a good sense of self
- □ Celebration of and respect for the differences between you
- □ Presence of valuing, listening, encouragement, interest and acceptance when your partner expresses needs, desires, aspirations, difficulties and feelings
- □ Absence of judgment, criticism, ridicule, 'put down' messages and rigidity
- □ Honest and open expression of your own needs, desires and ambitions, even when these run counter to those of your partner
- □ Active efforts to meet each other's needs

BEING SEPARATE IS WHAT MAKES A RELATIONSHIP

When couples attend for couple therapy, one of my primary tasks is to help them realise that they need to separate out from each other and see that as long as the identity of each is tied to the relationship, then conflict will continue. The separation issue is connected with helping each of them to find their own sense of self so that they may have greater independence of each other and begin to let go of their protectors, be they blaming self or partner, distancing strategies or binding strategies. These changes will create the foundation for the development of an unconditional loving relationship between them.

Separateness is an essential aspect of a fulfilling couple relationship. The paradox is that the more separate and independent you are, the deeper can be your involvement with another without loss of identity or individuality. An enmeshed relationship of opposites, where the healing opportunities are not seized upon, seriously blocks the unique identity of each partner and the growth of individuality and independence. In an enmeshed relationship any attempt by one partner to become independent is viewed by the other as a threat to the relationship and to their sense of self. Separateness is created through an intense, enduring and unconditional loving relationship with yourself. You cannot free yourself from enmeshment unless you first establish a safe and secure haven within yourself.

People sometimes misinterpret separateness as not needing anyone, but it is quite the opposite. Many social, emotional, sexual, financial, intellectual, occupational and physical needs are met in your relationship with your partner. Having a need is not dependence. When people are psychologically separate in their couple relationship, they will certainly express needs but will also accept that their partners have the freedom to say 'yes' or 'no' to the expressed need. Partners who are separate own and take responsibility for their individual needs. However, in a dependent relationship, a request is a command and a 'no' may be responded to with hostility, emotional or physical withdrawal, sulking, criticism and blaming. Clearly, if you are getting a lot of 'nos' to fair requests, then some deeper emotional block is operating and needs to be detected. There are all sorts of reasons why needs might not be met in a relationship: a feeling of not being loved, a feeling of being taken for granted, resentment over harsh criticism, suppressed anger arising from crucial needs not being seen, involvement with a third party, poor health, low self-esteem – the list is endless. The only way to find out what in particular is underlying the constant 'nos' is to enquire in a way that is not threatening. Likewise, if your partner never says 'no' to your requests, it would be wise to consider why this is so. It may well be that your partner is terrified of saying 'no', believes your needs are all-important or is living his life through you. Whether it is the situation of 'never a no' or 'always a no', there is clear evidence of an unhealthy alliance, the origins of which lie both in the present and in the past.

MOVING FROM PROTECTIVE TO OPEN WAYS OF RELATING

The power of opposites attracting

Protective ways of relating have the purpose of eliminating, or at least reducing, experiences of hurt and rejection. Protective strategies are not intentionally meant to block the relationship or abuse a partner but these may well be their effects. Each partner comes into the relationship with an armoury of protectors. However, it is only when the current protectors of one or both partners begin to weaken or cease to work that conflict will emerge between the couple.

It has been pointed out already that an amazing aspect of couple relationships is the phenomenon that opposites attract. The couple differ at the level of their protective strategies that guard against hurt and rejection. Remember there is wisdom in these strategies in that they serve the twofold purpose of protecting and alerting to the changes in behaviour needed to bring about the healing of old and present hurts. What is astounding in your choosing the opposite in protective behaviours to yourself is that your partner's behaviours signal the change in direction that your protective behaviours need to take and vice versa.

Of course in choosing an opposite you cleverly designed a further means of protecting yourself because an opposite behaviour is far

OPPOSING PROTECTIVE BEHAVIOURS

☐	Passive	Aggressive
☐	Dominant	Compliant
☐	Possessive	Elusive
☐	Overdemanding	Appeasing
☐	Perfectionist	Careless
☐	Manipulative	Blunt
☐	Introverted	Extroverted
☐	Emotionless	Histrionic
☐	Invasive	Aloof
☐	Selfish	Martyred
☐	Exhibitionist	Inhibited
☐	Cold	Overemotional
☐	Blaming	'Poor me'
☐	Pessimistic	Optimistic
☐	Logical	Overemotional
☐	Overconsiderate	Inconsiderate
☐	Hypersensitive	Insensitive
☐	Miserly	Spendthrift
☐	Wanting sameness	Wanting difference
☐	Secretive	Gossipy
☐	Oversexual	Asexual
☐	Ultra-responsible	Irresponsible
☐	Violent	Apathetic
☐	Panicky	Laid back
☐	Overserious	Comical
☐	Bottling up of feelings	Overexpressive of feelings
☐	Silent	Overtalkative
☐	Inferior	Superior

less threatening than the same one. Aggression breeds and threatens aggression but passivity colludes with and strengthens aggression. At a deeper healing level you chose an opposite so that when safe, you could avail of the opportunities for healing that exist in the relationship. The possibilities for healing will be taken up only when sufficient personal and interpersonal safety is present within and between the couple. Otherwise, the protective power of opposites attracting will be employed by both parties. If at any stage one set of protectors fails to offset hurt and rejection, either there will be an escalation of the present protective behaviours or new and stronger ones will be found. These may put too much pressure on the partner who is at the receiving end and conflict may ensue. The wisdom of the conflict is that the emotional perils may now be more readily seen, and remedial actions may be taken. Sometimes one or both of the partners may seek safety and support (professional or other) outside the relationship in order to tackle the relationship crisis and the longer term issues of personal vulnerabilities and childhood wounds.

You have already seen the types of protective relationships that can operate between two people. Depending on the level of vulnerability of the partners, protective strategies can range from mild to massively protective. Because opposites attract, it is useful to identify protective relationships according to the opposing types of relating that can exist between two people. As you read the list of opposing protective behaviours, keep in mind the power and the wisdom of these protectors as you begin to identify your own predominant patterns of relating.

This of course is not an exhaustive list. When you identify your own typical protectors and those of your partner, it is useful to ask yourself two questions; the answers will provide you with the origins of your present relationship difficulties:

- □ of which of my parents do my protective ways remind me?
- □ of which of my parents do my partner's protective ways remind me?

Remember that all these protective strategies have a double function: first, to reduce experiences of hurt, humiliation, failure and rejection, and, second, to alert you to the changes that are needed in you and your partner for progress to occur in each of you and between you. It is in this alerting function that the power of attraction between opposites lies.

Finding the golden mean between opposing protectors

The first step in letting go of protective ways is to discover your own typical protectors and the opposite, or sometimes similar, protections your partner uses. Then begin to employ the open and fair aspect of such bipolar behaviour. Let us take the example of the most common opposing behaviours of passivity and aggression: the partner who has been passive needs to learn the forceful and putting-yourself-forward aspects of aggression and to retain the respect-of-another aspect of passivity. The partner who has been aggressive needs to adopt a quieter, respectful but strong approach in expressing self. In fact, the middle ground between opposing behaviours is what both partners need to adopt. The middle-ground learning is essentially bipolar because it draws from both ends the best aspects of the opposing behaviours of the couple. The list below indicates the desirable bipolar evolution, or the golden mean, that occupies this middle ground.

The list of opposite ways of relating between partners is endless because of the ingenuity of human beings in protecting themselves in unsafe emotional, social and physical worlds. The couple relationship can be a powerful forum, not only for each of you to

OPPOSING PROTECTIVE BEHAVIOURS		GOLDEN MEAN
☐ Passive	Aggressive	Assertive
☐ Dominant	Compliant	Mindful of self and partner
☐ Possessive	Elusive	Taking hold and letting go
☐ Overdemanding	Appeasing	Expressing and responding to needs
☐ Perfectionist	Careless	Being careful and accepting of mistakes
☐ Manipulative	Blunt	'Up front' in a considerate way
☐ Introverted	Extroverted	Being able to be private and sociable
☐ Emotionless	Histrionic	Authentic
☐ Invasive	Aloof	Involvement with clear boundaries
☐ Selfish	Martyred	Mutual give-and-take
☐ Exhibitionist	Inhibited	Modest and outgoing
☐ Cold	Overemotional	Feelingful
☐ Blaming	'Poor me'	Owning your own needs
☐ Pessimistic	Optimistic	Realistic
☐ Logical	Overemotional	Rational and emotional
☐ Overconsiderate	Inconsiderate	Considerate
☐ Hypersensitive	Insensitive	Sensitive
☐ Miserly	Spendthrift	Thrifty
☐ Wanting sameness	Wanting difference	Challenge and stability
☐ Secretive	Gossipy	Discreet
☐ Oversexual	Asexual	Sexual

→

OPPOSING PROTECTIVE BEHAVIOURS		GOLDEN MEAN
□ Ultra-responsible	Irresponsible	Responsible
□ Violent	Apathetic	Strongly motivated
□ Panicky	Laid back	Alert
□ Overserious	Comical	Serious and humorous
□ Bottling up of feelings	Over-expressive of feelings	Mature expression of feelings
□ Silent	Overtalkative	Communicative and listening
□ Inferior	Superior	Self-confident

be truly free to be 'you', but also for the freedom to maturely express yourself along the continuum of all human ways of being.

It is only when you are under some physical, emotional or social threat that the extremes of a particular bipolar protective strategy will be employed to reduce or eliminate the threat. Within a safe relationship you will automatically adopt the golden mean between the bipolar extremes.

In Chapter 2 you identified which of your parents you find yourself repeating and which one is being repeated in your partner's protective ways. You and your partner now have the opportunity of creating a relationship with each other (and within yourselves) that neither of your parents, regrettably, achieved. In moving towards the golden mean between the opposing behaviours that exist in the relationship between you and your partner, you free yourself of the ties that bound you to your parents and unhealthily bound them to each other. You face the parent in your own protective ways of being with your partner and the parent in your partner's protective ways of being with you. The opportunities for emancipation from old ties and for individual growth and couple harmony are now very great.

When you begin to value, understand, learn from and confront the opposite protectors of your partner, you are already on the way to healing yourself and becoming more open in the relationship. But remember that this is a two-way street. Sadly, it is sometimes the case that one partner is ready and willing to go down the road of self-discovery, freedom from old ties, healing of past hurts and openness to a deeper and unconditional couple relationship, but the other partner remains locked in a dark cellar of insecurity and protective ways. Regrettably, the partner who is healing may have to progress alone down the road of psychological and social maturity and leave the trapped partner behind. The door of love and acceptance needs to remain open for the partner who is 'stuck' but not at the cost of your own personal and interpersonal development. Indeed, it would be an act of neglect to stay with the partner who refuses to seek help since your staying would be a collusion with the protector of avoidance of responsibility. There is a good chance that when the partner who is fearful of change sees your progress, he will find the safety to reach out for the help necessary to move out from the heavily protected dark space.

CHAPTER 9

RESOLVING CONFLICT

Don't find fault. Find a remedy.

Henry Ford

COUPLE CONFLICT IS CREATIVE

When conflicting couples come for therapy I often say to them 'oh happy conflict'. Very frequently they look at me with a 'jaundiced eye' since they may have just had a row before the session or have maintained a hostile silence for many days. Conflict is necessary and creative as it alerts you to the presence of hurts, vulnerabilities and ways of relating that need to be resolved within each partner as individuals and within the couple. If you view conflict as 'bad', then you may attempt to bury it, ignore it, blame your partner, family of origin or the world, hope that time will heal matters, or deny its existence. None of these responses will bring about the desired changes that the conflict between you is crying out for; indeed, the unresolved issues will only fester like an untreated wound. We are ready to accept that physical pain is a creative bodily force that signals some need for physical healing, but emotional and social pain are equally powerful signals that emotional healing is needed.

The first step in resolving couple conflict is the acceptance of the conflict and commitment to seizing the opportunities that it presents for healing and growing. The second step is to begin to identify the signs and sources of the conflict. A good starting-point for this process is to clarify precisely what aspects of the relationship are causing conflict. There may be one or several sources of disharmony:

- ☐ emotional sources
- ☐ physical sources
- ☐ behavioural sources
- ☐ social sources
- ☐ sexual sources.

Once you have identified the sources of conflict, the third step is to get behind the protection these sources provide to the real problem that has been hidden because it is too difficult to reveal.

Emotional sources of conflict

It is the emotional relating within the couple relationship that most needs to be explored. When this is conditional or of a hopeless and despairing nature, then all sorts of emotional difficulties will arise. Unconditional love is the deepest need of all human beings and its absence is the cause of many couple problems. Clearly the nature, intensity, frequency and duration of lack of loving will determine the level of couple disharmony. Emotional problems in a relationship can manifest themselves in a myriad of ways. Very often the real issue of not feeling loved by your partner is camouflaged. For example, severe conditions like anorexia nervosa or bulimia can often hide a starvation of love or a deep need to be fed affection. Cancer phobias can be metaphors for the dis-ease of not feeling wanted in a relationship. Abdominal pain is often an indicator of a fear of not being loved. Sometimes years of treatment for such symptoms do not reduce the severity of the complaints because there has been no shift in the underlying issue of needing to be loved by your partner.

Below are some of the more common signs of emotional conflict. Hold onto the realisation that the manifestation of conflict is a protective device and not in itself the problem. The problem lies deeper within the person or between the couple; generally both. You can be sure that the problem lies around the issue of love.

Many emotional difficulties of couples manifest themselves through sexual behaviours. This may be so because sex is the one biological drive that is social in nature and is not life-threatening when you deny it to your partner. At least 60 per cent of psycho-sexual problems are due to deeper identity and intimacy issues within the couple relationship. Little change in the sexual lives of partners will occur unless there is a deeper understanding of and response to the hidden emotional conflicts. For example, a man's sexual impotency may be a manifestation of his sense of power-lessness around women. A woman's difficulty in allowing pene-tration may be a revelation of her fear of intimacy and closeness or of repressed sexual abuse experienced in childhood.

One of the most commonly presenting emotional problems between partners is a female partner complaining 'he never shows any warmth or affection', 'he's incapable of feeling anything', 'he only wants me for sex' or 'I never know what he's feeling'. This is a difficult relationship in which your prime need to be loved and wanted is not being met. Whatever the reason for your partner's protective coldness – the answer nearly always lies in a loveless home of origin – change has to occur in this fundamental issue if you are to be able to continue in the relationship. Of course you will need to look at what attracted you to this person in the first place. It is possible that you have become involved with a person like the parent who did not show you affection. On the one hand, there is great protection in living with someone who does not make emotional demands on you, particularly if you doubt your own

SIGNS OF EMOTIONAL CONFLICT BETWEEN PARTNERS

☐ Psychosomatic signs	• Arthritis • back pain • anorexia nervosa • bulimia • tension headaches • fatigue • abdominal pain • hypertension • stomach ulcers
☐ Behavioural signs	• Threats • aggression • blaming • violence • physical withdrawal • clinging • possessiveness • perfectionism • passivity • impulsiveness • overspending • stealing • being absent from home • overworking
☐ Emotional signs	• Coldness • jealousy • fearfulness • isolation • loneliness • guilt • depression • bottling up of feelings • rejection • irritability • emotional outbursts • overexpression of feelings of love, caring and attention
☐ Cognitive signs	• Overabsorption in interests and hobbies • denial of problems • intellectualising of emotional problems • obsessions with cleanliness, values or religion • 'living in your head' • worrying all the time • depressive thought patterns • 'living in the future' • 'living in the past'
☐ Social signs	• Few or no social outings together • few or no invitations to outsiders • long periods of silence between couple • shyness • overtalkativeness • social phobias of meeting people • non-assertiveness • allowing unwelcome intrusions by others • non-listening
☐ Sexual signs	• Little or no sexual contact • dislike of touching intimate parts of partner's body • premature ejaculation • dislike of own body • hating sex • vaginismus • being non-orgasmic • deviant sexual practices

lovability. On the other hand, you get the opportunity to face the mother within yourself that accepted a loveless relationship and the father in your husband. You can now assert (it would have been too threatening as a child to do this to your father) that you deserve to be shown love and warmth. Most male partners will respond to this request, particularly when you take it to its action conclusion – no loving, no relationship. Your partner will need your support to seek the help that he needs to find the safety to be able to express his feelings. But the rewards for this effort can be a more mature partner and a more fulfilling emotional relationship.

Resolution of a couple's emotional difficulties can be a lengthy process since the problems not only stretch back to the families of origin, but also involve current self-image and ideal self issues, non-separation from parents and a co-dependent relationship.

In my experience of working with couples, the following are essential aspects of emotional healing:

- Separation of each partner from family of origin (Chapter 3)
- Establishment of own separate identity by each partner (Chapter 4)
- Establishment by each partner of separateness from each other (Chapter 8)
- Creation of emotional and physical safety for each partner to be different (Chapter 8)
- Development of an unconditionally loving, supportive, valuing, respectful, fair, just and friendly relationship with each other (Chapter 10)
- Provision by each partner of affirmation, support and encouragement for the development of a sense of worth in each other (Chapter 5)
- Awareness always that conflicts are opportunities for change within the individual partners and within the relationship (present chapter)

Physical sources of conflict

Sometimes conflict arises in a couple relationship because a partner is ill, tired, overstretched, burnt out and in need of medical attention, rest or some relief from responsibilities. The issue underlying the physical problem may be an addiction to work or perfectionism. These issues will need to be corrected if harmony is to be restored to the relationship. Very often the partners of perfectionists never feel the home is theirs because of undue demands for tidiness and order. Equally, the partner who is involved with someone whose job dominates his life will often feel deserted and experience feelings of rejection because she feels that his work is more important than her or their relationship. Establishment of a fair balance between the needs of the couple relationship and work is required.

Violence is an all-too-common source of couple disharmony. It is an indictment of our society that at least one in five women experience violence in their marriages. It is important to state that women also can be violent towards their partners, but female violence is far less prevalent. No matter what the source of violence – whether deep personal insecurity, relentless demands from one's partner, excessive alcohol intake or fatigue – it cannot be tolerated in any shape or form. Violence powerfully undermines the dignity of the victim and perpetuates the deep problems of the perpetrator. In too many cases of physical abuse, women excuse its occurrence and are deluded by profuse apologies into believing that it will never occur again. This is rarely the case and no woman (or man) should tolerate a second beating. Seek refuge, procure a protection order, speak out to relatives and professionals and be very clear that unless your partner seeks the help that he needs, you will not return to the profound unsafety of your couple relationship. You deserve to be loved and respected and to feel safe in this world. Do not let anybody deprive you of these rights.

Sometimes couple conflict may have a physical source arising from physical incapacity due to illness, accident, a psychosomatic condition (for example, asthma, high blood pressure) or agoraphobia (fear of open spaces). When one partner is physically incapacitated, this can be an enormous disappointment to the other partner and can place an intolerable burden of caring on her shoulders. It also means that it may not be possible to meet many of the needs that are part and parcel of the couple relationship.

Other physical bases for conflict include financial strain, one partner being miserly or one not exercising desirable thrift, restricted living accommodation, living with in-laws, living next to hostile neighbours or living in an unsafe location.

In relationships that are relatively harmonious, a couple will normally resolve these difficulties. However, in insecure relationships, these problems either go unnoticed or are reacted to with impatience, irritability or withdrawal. Consequently the conflict increases and sometimes has to reach 'screaming point' – serious illness, physical breakdown, escalation of violence – before a couple will seek help. Even then it may be that only one of the partners seeks help and support whilst the other remains locked behind the steel doors of denial. All the time the function of the conflict is to produce development and growth.

Behavioural sources of conflict

What you do and don't do, what you say and don't say, are windows into the inner world of yourself and the outer world of your relationships with others, work and the material universe. We reveal vulnerability in a myriad of behavioural ways – the way you walk into a room, level of eye contact, shyness, passivity and hot-headedness are just some of these indicators. Some couples possess poor or no behavioural control of self or of interactions with each other. A partner may complain: 'he never allows me make any decisions', 'he shouts me down all the time', 'he has to have his own way all the time', 'he never washes himself', 'he always expects me to clean up after him', 'he never lets me know when he's going to be late home', 'she's never home', 'she never cooks a meal', 'she overspends' – the possibilities are countless. Though these behavioural responses are the overt source of the problem, they are a protective mask for the more hidden issues of fears of rejection and of unresolved old hurts and vulnerabilities.

I recall one woman who complained that her husband rarely washed himself, but he would still expect her to make love and to sleep with him. She continued to blame him until I gently asked her to explore why she was colluding with his neglect of himself and of her by having sex with him and sleeping in the same bed. She began to see that she did not have enough respect for herself and feared his rejection if she said 'no' to him. Only when she began to say 'no' did he choose to come for help. Up to that point he was able to hide behind the protection of her collusion.

People tend to recognise 'out-of-control' actions as manifestations of lack of discipline but it is important to recognise that 'overcontrolled' behaviour is also a lack of behavioural responsibility. Passivity is as much a neglect of the well-being of each partner and the relationship as is aggression. As a therapist I have helped couples where the male partner, who expressed his insecurities through out-of-control actions, was seen as 'the devil' and the female partner, who manifested her vulnerability through overcontrolled behaviours, was deemed 'a saint'. The distinction between these two sets of behaviours is important as both result in serious blocking of development of the partners as individuals and as a couple. Too much violence has been perpetuated by 'a blind eye being turned'. An equally serious act of neglect is for any woman or man not to assert and act on their rights to be loved, respected and allowed to pursue their goals in life without fear and intimidation. Changing overcontrolled responses to conflict is just as crucial as altering out-of-control ones. Examples of these types of responses are given below.

OUT-OF-CONTROL BEHAVIOURS	OVERCONTROLLED BEHAVIOURS
☐ Threatening	☐ Silence
☐ Shouting	☐ Withdrawal
☐ Screaming	☐ Lack of initiative
☐ Hitting	☐ Passivity
☐ Pushing	☐ 'Turning a blind eye'
☐ Grabbing	☐ Non-confrontation
☐ Shoving	☐ Sulking
☐ Being careless	☐ Apathy
☐ Poor hygiene	☐ Overpleasing
☐ Neglect of property	☐ Rarely saying 'no'
☐ Overeating	☐ Bottling up feelings
☐ Overdrinking	☐ Perfectionism
☐ Dominating	☐ Covering up neglect by partner
☐ Controlling	☐ Being secretive
☐ Blaming	☐ Blaming self for partner's out-of-control actions
☐ Criticising	

Inevitably, when a couple are either overreacting or under-reacting to each other, there are emotional bases to the conflict which have to be resolved. However, change at the level of behaviour is also important, so that there is some behavioural safety for the couple to explore the deeper emotional sources of their difficulties. The absence of violence, criticism, ridicule, 'put-down' messages, sarcasm, cynicism, hostile silences, sulking and physical withdrawal makes it easier to establish the presence of love, respect, valuing, affirmation, praise, care, listening, compassion, understanding, humour and fairness between the troubled couple.

Social sources of conflict

The source of some couple conflict lies in such social deficits as 'she never wants to go out anywhere', 'he hates having people in', 'he disappears when people come to the house', 'he never makes the effort to talk to me or others', 'he never wants to come away on holidays with me', 'he expects me to go to the same pub every time we go out', 'she spends more time with her mother than she does with me', 'he always has to be the centre of attention', 'when we go out together, he leaves me sitting on my own and spends most of the time talking to friends'. These social sources of conflict typically arise from deeper emotional issues, more particularly a lack of self-confidence. These deficit or excess social behaviours may also be signs of serious emotional distancing between the partners and, accordingly, require serious reflection on the relationship.

Some social deficits or excesses arise directly from a lack of sensitivity to the social needs of a partner while others reflect just a plain lack of interpersonal skills. As regards a lack of sensitivity, it is important that the partner who feels socially let down by her partner lets him know calmly and clearly what her social needs are rather than assuming that he should know himself. As regards the issue of the partner who lacks social skills, it would be important that he owns this deficit and sets about acquiring such skills. There are many books and courses on the acquisition of social, communication and assertiveness skills. A course on self-esteem would also benefit this partner.

The phenomenon of stereotyping has led many men to believe that the place for their female partners is in the bed, kitchen and church. These men, and very often their partners, do not appear to realise that women need social stimulation for their personal development. The man who is threatened by the social emancipation of his partner is masking doubts about himself and fears of losing his partner. The more emancipated a partner is, the greater the possibilities for a lasting couple relationship. Research has shown that housebound women are far more prone to depression and dissatisfaction with their lives than those women who, along with their family commitments, have career and social outlets.

Lack of social outings and regular times for the couple to talk and listen to each other, plan together, reflect together, cook together, watch television together, have friends in for a meal and share domestic responsibilities does not augur well for the intimate development of the relationship. The more a couple interact with one another, the greater the cohesiveness and closeness.

Other social sources of conflict may be living with in-laws or having to care for an elderly parent. Living with in-laws should be avoided as much as possible; when it is unavoidable, distinct boundaries need to be established and communicated directly and clearly to the parents. Of course it is also important to hear where their boundaries lie. A son or daughter who is still enmeshed with parents will find it extremely difficult to confront the parents on these issues. If this is the case, then some outside help may be required to arm this son or daughter with self-respect, separateness from parents and determination to give priority to the couple relationship. If the parents remain hostile, difficult and invasive, in spite of repeated overt requests, it is best for the young couple to find their own living accommodation as soon as possible. It is not a material inheritance that brings happiness to a relationship but being there for each other.

When there is an elderly parent who requires some assistance, it is important that a fair sharing of the caring responsibilities occurs. When there are other sons or daughters, meetings need to be arranged regularly to discuss who will do what. If the parent who needs caring is uncooperative and dominant, it is important not to collude with such disrespect and to let your actions show this clearly.

Social interactions are a major determinant of the quality of a relationship. A close relationship would need to include the following kinds of social contact on a regular basis:

- Interest in each other
- Listening
- Talking over your day's experiences
- Helping each other
- Sharing responsibilities
- Outings together
- Dinner parties
- Humour
- Playing games together
- Problem-solving together
- Planning
- Remembering birthdays, anniversaries
- 'Out of the blue' thoughtfulness
- Giving gifts
- Sensitivity to each other's feelings

Sexual sources of conflict

It has already been pointed out that a high percentage of sexual problems within a relationship are due to underlying relationship problems and even deeper self-image and ideal self difficulties.

However, some sexual problems are purely a matter of lack of knowledge, where the couple do not know ways to sexually pleasure each other. In this situation, an increase in sexual expertise can greatly enhance the sexual relationship. Numerous books and videos are now available on this subject.

However, far more serious sexual problems than simply lack of knowledge can exist in a couple relationship. The more common problems for men are premature ejaculation, partial or complete impotency, retarded ejaculation (cannot climax despite an erection) and situational impotency. The more common problems among women are being non-orgasmic, vaginismus (involuntary contraction of the vaginal muscles making penetration painful or impossible) and situational inorgasmia. Psychosexual problems common to both sexes include loss of libido, total disinterest in sex, guilt, fear of causing pain, fear of pregnancy and repulsion to sexual secretions or sexual organs.

When inorgasmia in women or impotency in men is situational – meaning that she or he can reach a sexual climax outside the couple relationship – then the problem lies in their couple relationship. Attendance with either a psychotherapist or psychosexual counsellor is then needed to resolve both the emotional and sexual problems. Most other sexual problems stem from childhood experiences where sex was taboo or sexual abuse was experienced or punishment was meted out for sexual explorations. It is not the domain of this book to go into the resolution of these problems, but there are many books on this topic.

Sexual problems – except possibly where there is non-consummation of the relationship, sexual deviance (such as transvestism, masochism, sado-masochism) or major sexual differences (one partner is homosexual and the other heterosexual) – are rarely the cause of the breakdown of a couple relationship.

However, many long-term relationships seem to experience a gradual loss of interest in sex. This can be a serious loss, particularly when one of the partners has not experienced such a diminution in sexual desire. When this is the case, clear communication and efforts to revitalise sexual activity are required. Otherwise an extra-relationship affair is likely.

Communication on sexual matters does not come easily to many couples. This is not surprising given the double messages society gives about sexual behaviour: it is wonderful but not something you talk about openly. Religious indoctrination has done serious damage to people's concepts of their bodies and physical intimacy. Parents still rarely talk to children about sex. Furthermore, because of the emphasis on 'the body beautiful' by an exploitative cosmetic industry, many men and women have deep physical self-image difficulties. This sensitivity, coupled with the notion that you should be a wonderful lover (in spite of lack of education, myths about sexuality and negative indoctrination), can make talking about sexual difficulties highly threatening to individual partners.

A frequent complaint by women in the sexual arena of a couple relationship is that 'he is overdemanding sexually, wanting it two, three times a day'. Some women have difficulties in saying 'no' to these partners, even though they may feel definitely not interested in sexual contact at certain times. A woman is not responsible for her partner's sexual needs – that is his responsibility. It is therefore important that she communicates in a loving but clear way when she feels uncomfortable and when she feels not in the mood for sexual involvement: 'I'm tired right now and do not feel like making love', 'I'm in the middle of my period and I don't feel comfortable in my body', 'I do find it difficult that you request having sex so often', 'I do not seem to have the same level of need', 'can we agree that it is okay for me to say "yes" or "no" to your sexual request?'

Some women fear that they will lose their partners if they are not always responsive, but the contrary is more likely. When you go against yourself, resentment and emotional distancing are likely to develop, leading to far more serious problems. Moreover your partner will feel your reticence in the sexual encounter and may misinterpret it as rejection. Furthermore sexual contact will be far more fulfilling when both of you really want it. Clearly when either party is minimally responsive to the other's sexual needs, then serious discussion is required.

One final issue is that many couples do not make their sexual lives a priority: it tends to be given time and space when everything else has been done and both partners are tired and stressed out. This is a recipe for sexual disharmony. It is important that sexual spontaneity is not hampered, but making 'dates', taking the phone off the hook, having a romantic dinner for two or taking an afternoon off all help the process of sexual harmony.

TALKING THROUGH CONFLICT

When safe, talk

Whether the signs of conflict are physical, behavioural, emotional, social or sexual – or some combination of these – it is essential that a couple get down to talking about it. Where each of the parties to a troubled relationship has a moderate degree of self-possession and there exists a fair level of interpersonal safety between them, it is likely that issues will get voiced.

When you decide to talk out what is troubling you about the relationship, it might help to consider the following suggestions:

- Listen to yourself
- Own the difficulties you wish to express

- Select an appropriate time
- Request that your partner listens without interruption
- Reassure your partner that what you are about to say is about you and your needs, worries and concerns, and not a criticism of him
- Send 'I' messages
- Do not bring up old grievances
- Stick to the immediate conflict issues
- Stay separate from your partner's protective responses
- Do your best to stay in charge of self and do not be drawn into arguing
- Listen when your partner responds respectfully

The first act of communication is to listen to yourself so that you are strongly in touch with your emotional and behavioural responses to the difficult aspects of the relationship. When you talk, it is vital that you talk about yourself and not about your partner. For example, if you complain 'you're always out' you are not owning your own need and your partner is likely to protectively react to your judgment and criticism. However, if you own and take responsibility for the troublesome issue, your communication may now take the form: 'I really miss you when you're not at home in the evening times' or 'I am worried that you are not spending time at home' or 'When you don't come home after work, I am afraid that you have lost interest in our relationship.' Owning the issue makes it more likely that your partner will stay open to what you are revealing; not owning is likely to produce the contrary response.

The timing of your approach to your partner about an issue that undoubtedly will be threatening to him is an important consideration. An ideal time is when there is closeness and intimacy between you and there is sufficient time to raise the matters of conflict. In deeply troubled relationships, the possibility of the existence of such intimate opportunities is remote, because a whole range of distancing strategies may be operating. Nevertheless some time needs to be chosen when the partner is not tired, does not have excess alcohol taken, is not rushing out, the time-span is not limited, and other people are not present or likely to visit. Be sure you consider how you are feeling yourself. It is not wise to emotionally explode with an issue since the only responses open to your partner are either to run for cover or to attack back, neither of which provides the safe forum for you to continue voicing your difficulties. Hold onto the fact that your partner is not responsible for your happiness and be as self-possessed as possible before the confrontation.

A request on your part for your partner to listen without interruption may smooth the path ahead, particularly when that request is followed by the reassurance that what is to follow is about you and not in any way a criticism of him. When your partner lacks a strong sense of self, this reassurance of being non-judgmental may need to be repeated a number of times before he internalises the message.

The basis of sound confrontation is the 'I' message; unfortunately it is far more common for partners to send 'you' messages to each other. Whilst a 'you' message escapes being indirect (an indirect message being one that is not directed to anyone in particular), its meaning is always unclear (as the message sent seems to be about the receiver and not the sender). A clear message, on the other hand, is always about some feeling, need or opinion of the sender. For example, when a partner says 'you never tell me you love me' the communication is direct (it is addressed to the partner) but unclear and it is left to the receiver to interpret the message as saying something about his partner. A possible interpretation would be 'I'm feeling insecure about our relationship and would like to be reassured that you still love me.' A direct and clear communication from the sender could have emerged as 'I do need for you to let me know at times that you love me.' However, when you are vulnerable a 'you' message is a clever device in that it reduces emotional risk-taking and possible hurt. It is a protective means of communication in that all the responsibility for what you are feeling is transferred onto the partner being confronted. Examples are:

- □ 'You make me so unhappy.'
- □ 'You're never here when I need you.'
- □ 'You only think of yourself.'
- □ 'You never listen.'
- □ 'You think you know it all.'
- □ 'How could you do such a thing?'

The sender of these messages takes no emotional risk (since the communication is unclear and no need is expressed) but their effect is to threaten greatly the receiver and lead him to protectively retort: 'you're always complaining' or 'you're like a non-stop record' or 'you're full of shit.' No progress in resolving the conflict between the couple can now occur. The wisdom and strength of the 'I' message is that you as the sender own totally what you want to say, the message is non-critical and non-judgmental and the message is direct and abundantly clear. Taking the examples above, the 'I' format could be:

- □ 'I'm feeling unhappy with our lovemaking and need you to respect my "no" about certain requests you make of me.'
- □ 'I feel let down and upset when you're not there to support me through the difficulties I'm having at work.'

- ▫ 'I need you to listen to and consider my needs as well as your own.'
- ▫ 'I feel invisible and angry when you do not listen to my way of seeing things.'
- ▫ 'I believe my opinions are worthy of respect and I feel hurt when you are dismissive of them.'
- ▫ 'I am aware that I did not communicate my need for confidentiality on aspects of our relationship but I did feel angry when I heard these issues being repeated by your sister.'

A frequently employed protective strategy is for one or both parties to delve into the past and resurrect old hurts and wrongdoings, thereby cleverly distracting from the immediate issue that is threatening self and the relationship. Like a broken record, the partner who is confronting needs to keep reiterating the behaviours that are currently causing distress. You also need to keep things in perspective and see that your partner's protective responses – whether it is going into the museum of old grievances, over-intellectualising or rationalising, or attempting to put you down – are all revelations of his vulnerability. You cannot be deterred from the path to bringing your relationship to the more firm ground of fairness, justice and true intimacy. Finally, when your partner does respectfully respond to your grievances, the same courtesies of listening to and valuing his viewpoints need to be accorded to him. It is from this base of mutual listening and valuing that progress can be made towards meeting the needs of both partners.

When unsafe, seek support

When past experiences of attempting to 'talk things over' have been met by strong protective responses – verbal or physical aggression, hostile withdrawal and silence, or manipulative reactions of histrionics, 'taking to the bottle', 'taking to the bed', overdosing on pills, not eating for days or endless days of sulking – then it is safer to say nothing. You recognise that these extreme reactions of your partner mirror his deep insecurity and are attempts to control you so that you do not make demands that threaten the status quo. In saying nothing, the conflict remains and is guaranteed to mushroom. However, saying nothing does not mean doing nothing about the untenable situation. Because it is both physically and emotionally unsafe, it is now necessary to go outside the relationship to voice the difficulties so that you can obtain emotional support and even direct help in confronting your partner on the blocks that exist in the relationship between you. Confrontation is an act of caring for both yourself and your partner. Neither he nor you deserves to have legitimate needs unheeded in the relationship. Furthermore, confrontation offers both of you the safe ground to emerge from behind the protective walls of resistance to change. With confrontation, each partner and the relationship gain; with silence, matters get worse.

Before you choose to talk to somebody other than your partner, be sure to look first to yourself. Many people who have sought help for their relationship difficulties see their partners as having all the problems; if he would only change, all would be well! Problems marry problems and relationship difficulties demand changes in both partners. Ask yourself the following questions:

☐ Is my love unconditional?
☐ Do I send 'I' messages?
☐ Do I listen?
☐ Am I tolerant of differences between us?
☐ Do I consider my partner's needs?
☐ Am I overconsiderate and protective?
☐ Do I sulk, withdraw or maintain hostile silences?

- □ Do I nag?
- □ Do I shout, roar and scream?
- □ Am I judgmental and critical?

If you answer 'no' to any of the first five questions or 'yes' to any of the remaining ones, you have some indication of the self and interpersonal work that you yourself need to do. It is wise that you take the stye from your own eye before confronting the one in your partner's.

When you have taken at least some account of your own vulnerability and your contribution to the troubled couple relationship, select a person to talk to with whom you feel emotionally safe and who will listen, be discreet, be non-judgmental and, on request, be able to provide sound advice. Having such a support person may help you to devise means of confronting your partner about your unhappiness. Possible strategies are:

- □ Write to your partner
- □ Give him an audio-tape of your concerns
- □ Request somebody he respects to talk to him

When there is no response to such overtures, stronger measures may be required; actions always speak louder than words.

When partner remains 'stuck', move

You deserve a fulfilling relationship. When you know that your partner is fully aware of your dissatisfactions but is not demonstrating any fair and just response, then a range of possible actions are open to you. Be sure that these actions are taken within a climate of unconditional positive regard. It is the behaviour and not the person of your partner that is the problem.

- ☐ Move to separate bedroom
- ☐ Break the silence on the difficulties to both sides of the family
- ☐ Attend counsellor for self and offer same to partner
- ☐ Leave home and go to stay with somebody who is supportive
- ☐ Send a solicitor's letter
- ☐ Where there is intimidation or violence, report it to your medical practitioner and police, seek refuge and obtain a protection order from the District Court

Frequently, when any one of these actions is taken, your partner will show an escalation of old protective devices of aggression, control, manipulation or silent treatment. When these are seen not to deflect you from your course of action, a switch may occur to alternative compensatory behaviours of weeping and promising all sorts of changes – once you come back. It would be unwise to relinquish your present course of action in response to these verbalisations. Certainly acknowledge that this is what you want in the relationship, but let him know that until there are clear visible signs of change extending over a period of time, you do not feel safe enough to let go of your proactions. Furthermore, your partner needs to be left with no doubt that should he return to his old ways, you will reinstate your actions to regain emotional safety and the freedom to pursue your goals in life.

A good index of a partner's willingness and readiness to change is his agreement to attend for either individual or couple counselling. Resistance to such suggestions may result in simply a short-lived return to a blissful reunion. Whether or not your partner changes, it is vital that you continue on your path towards greater personal security and independence and continue your search for a relationship that is celebratory of you.

WHEN HELP IS NEEDED

There are couples who require help to refind intimacy or discover it for the first time in their relationship. These couples may seek help when too much pain and hurt are occurring, when their protectors against each other's power to hurt and control are no longer holding, when one of the partners has found some personal security and outside emotional support to reach out for professional help, when refuge from violence has been sought, or when children are at risk.

There are many reasons why couples may not be in a position to resolve their own difficulties and attain closeness with each other:

☐ Protective forces are extreme (for example, violence, endless silence, denial of problems, addiction to alcohol or drugs, endless verbal arguments, extreme physical and emotional withdrawal)
☐ Deep-seated personal problems needing professional help (for example, depression, hallucinations, delusions, obsessive-compulsive behaviours, chronic generalised anxiety)
☐ Very low self-image, unrealistic ideal self or no ideals at all in one or both partners
☐ Extreme co-dependence
☐ Repressive family background
☐ Extreme non-separation from family of origin
☐ Lack of support systems outside the couple relationship
☐ One partner being financially dependent on the other

It is always revealing which of the partners first seeks professional help or suggests therapy for both of them. It is not always the case that the partner who first requests help is the more motivated to change. In my experience, sometimes the initiator of the consultation is seeking an ally in the therapist in order to lay blame on the other partner. When this does not transpire, the initiating partner may withdraw from therapy, begin to miss appointments or denigrate the therapist to the other partner. The protective ploy of securing an ally has not worked and there is a threat now that the previously reluctant partner may gain from the therapy. All these responses indicate the depth of fear, denial and insecurity in the initiating partner, and an effective therapist will do their best to make it safe for this client to persevere in therapy.

In spite of the best efforts of the therapist, there are situations where one partner drops out of therapy. Once again there are many possible reasons behind this major protective device:

- The partner is having an extra-marital relationship
- Fear that secrets (such as sexual abuse, sexual deviance, addictions) may be discovered
- Fear of rejection by therapist and partner when hidden vulnerabilities and past traumatic experiences are revealed
- Addiction to alcohol or drugs
- Fear of failure
- No longer possesses love feelings for partner
- Is repulsed by partner
- Never wanted to be married
- Sees therapy as being there for the partner but not for self

It is important that if your partner drops out of therapy (and the reasons are not always clear) you do not feel obliged to follow suit. This would only reinforce the avoidance of your partner and send the relationship back to square one. When you remain in therapy, you have an opportunity to explore what brought you into this troubled relationship, what has led you to live with such unhappiness for so long, where you are in terms of your own relationship with yourself and your parents, and how you can now redeem yourself and possibly the couple relationship. Lots of reasons to stay in therapy! The attendance of both partners is not essential to couple therapy, though it certainly is more desirable. My own experiences of helping distressed couples is that change in one party inevitably brings about a change in the other – not, of course, always in the direction of maturity. But even an escalation in protectiveness is a movement and shows the partner attending therapy how even more expedient it is to stay in therapy. When both partners are motivated, considerable changes at all levels of conflict can be achieved.

Because there are several levels of conflict to be dealt with in couple therapy, it is wise to check out the credentials and experience of the therapist to whom you are referred. Word of mouth or recommendation by your medical practitioner are generally reliable referral sources. The recommendation is that the professional who practises couple therapy would have at least a doctorate in clinical psychology, psychotherapy, psychoanalysis or family therapy. This is necessary advice because when a couple presents for help the therapist needs to possess the expertise to work at all the levels of conflict: between the couple, from the couple's families of origin and within each of them as individuals. Where there are children, family difficulties are certain to have evolved and need resolving. Sometimes the children may need individual help as well. Of course, being professionally qualified does not necessarily mean that the therapist will be effective. What applies to the medical profession – 'doctors differ, patients die' – I am sure is true also of psychologists and psychotherapists. Nevertheless, there is some protection in credentials.

When a couple or one of the partners feels uncomfortable with a particular therapist, it is important that either this is voiced or another therapist is selected. However, be wary of the possibility that you or your partner may be setting up therapists to fail (particularly when a number of therapists have failed to fit the bill); such failure on the part of therapists protects you from the threats that change would pose were therapy to be successful.

There is a notion that couple therapy is successful only when a reconciliation is achieved. However, a decision to leave a relationship may be what is really needed for one of the partners so that she can truly recommence her life's journey. Certainly, when one of the partners either protectively refuses to come for help or protectively sabotages any therapeutic intervention and stays 'stuck' in a bitter cycle of defensive behaviours, then a decision to leave is mature. Sometimes a decision to part may be made in spite of attaining a reconciliation, greater personal security, separateness and independence. This can happen with a couple who married very young and who, when they enter therapy fifteen to twenty years later, have very much 'fallen out of love' with each other. It is very difficult to rekindle the embers of a cold fire. A friendship may be possible, but not intimacy.

The main purpose of couple therapy is for the therapist to create the emotional safety for each of the partners and both together that they have been unable to create among themselves. It is only through the light of emotional safety, love, acceptance, compassion, understanding and the guidance of the therapist that the dark shadows of the phenomenal protectors of distressed couples can be penetrated. It can be a long painful process, but one that brings in its train joy, healing, growing, independence, separateness and, it is hoped, intimacy between the partners. When a couple do not pursue or stay on the therapeutic road, sadly, they will continue to tread the path of darkness, despair and living in personal and interpersonal worlds in which neither of them have found what we all most desire – intimacy.

PART V

ENDPOINT

Enduring Feeling

When the light fades
to shade
what's unseen
may still be there

When the dark sights
sunlight
what is seen
may not be there

Whether it's night
or light
what I feel
is always there

Tony Humphreys

CHAPTER 10

INTIMACY

A good marriage is that in which each appoints
the other guardian of his solitude.

Rainer Maria Rilke

BRINGING IT ALL TOGETHER

This book has attempted to show that couples do not start out with a clean slate when they become involved with each other. On the contrary, there are many issues inscribed on their individual slates – the emotional baggage from their childhoods – that will play a major role in the formation, maintenance and development of their relationship. It is fascinating to see that your choice of partner was already being formed in the early years of your childhood, and that each of your parents' relationship with you and their relationship with each other will greatly influence how you behave in your relationship with your partner. What is even more wondrous is that the couple relationship offers the most far-reaching opportunities for healing the hurts of the past and for the mature development of each of the partners and the relationship itself.

The couple relationship has the potential to become the safe forum for the discovery of your own goodness and worth and that of your partner and for the experience of an enduring and unconditional loving relationship. In marrying your father or mother (or a person who is diametrically opposed in behaviour to either of your parents), you have the opportunity to redeem your lost or poor sense of self in your relationship with your partner. In securing his love and acceptance you can heal the relationship between you and the parent who most hurt and abandoned you. In the mirror of his love for you, you can also begin to love and accept yourself, and from this solid and secure base risk loving your partner. In being attracted to the opposite to yourself, you can learn the more moderate and desirable aspects of your partner's ways of living that will aid your journey of healing yourself, separating out from your family of origin and committing yourself to an open and unconditional relationship with your partner. The healing opportunities that are there for you are also there for your partner because you represent his most powerful chance for change.

There are none of us who do not have issues to resolve from childhood. Equally there is no couple relationship that is not burdened by the hurts of the past and the individual vulnerability of each partner in the present. Each of us has a responsibility to heal the hurt child within, to separate out from dependence on parents and family of origin, and to develop the most powerful and enduring relationship of all – our relationship with self. It is this relationship that provides the separateness and independence that is required for the survival and continual growth of a couple relationship. Regrettably, it is the relationship that has been most neglected in our culture, but it is the rock on which to build all other relationships.

The relationship with self and the development of an open and mature relationship with a partner are the bedrock of a healthy family. Children need parents who love themselves and love each other – these relationships model for children how they can be within themselves and with others. Even more importantly, children whose parents have achieved or are on the road to achieving an acceptance of self and of each other experience an enduring unconditional loving from these parents. The emotional baggage that these children as adults will carry into their intimate relationships will be indeed light.

This book has brought you on the journey of the formation and development of a couple relationship. The most important milestones along that journey are:

▫ How your parents were with you
▫ How your parents related to each other
▫ How you now see yourself
▫ How you now see your parents and family of origin

If you have not resolved issues arising from these milestones before entering an intimate relationship with another, you will have chosen the perfect partner for you to tackle these unresolved conflicts. Other milestones along the path to intimacy will now begin to appear:

▫ You chose the perfect partner
▫ The power of opposites attracting
▫ How you see yourself in the relationship
▫ How your partner sees you
▫ Couple conflict is creative

The challenges for change within yourself, the healing of the child within and the availing of the opportunities that the relationship offers for healing now become urgent issues, particularly when the protectors against hurt and rejection begin to weaken. Respect, value and see the wisdom of each other's protectors. At the same time see the alerting message of a protective response and know that unless emotional safety is created, you and your partner need to protect each from the other. Compassion, patience, encouragement and most of all unconditional love are the hallmarks of emotional safety which provides the forum for healing and change.

WHAT LOVE IS

The essence of intimacy is unconditional love which is shown in empathic relating. This relating involves unconditional love of your partner for his unique person and being, and not for anything he does. Such loving is a giving to give rather than to get. Conditional loving is a manipulation to get the other person to be what you want: it is a denial and rejection of your partner's uniqueness and right to be different from you. It is seeing your partner as being there for you. The empathic couple, on the other hand, celebrate each other, allow for the unique growth of each other and provide as best they can the emotional environment and resources for such growth. The couple who are empathic come into their relationship with a sense of the wonder of their own beings and a realisation of their behavioural limitations. These partners do not impose their own views on each other but are sensitive to the different needs of each other. They show interest in each other's thoughts, feelings, interests, hobbies, career, spiritual beliefs, philosophy of life and friendships because they love each other.

There are no conditions for love in the empathic couple relationship. In such a partnership, the relationship comes first and always comes before differences and issues relating to domestic responsibilities. When confrontation is required regarding some behaviour that is threatening or unacceptable, it is always done within the context of the loving relationship: for example, 'I love you but I am unhappy with you comparing me to your mother' or 'our relationship is important to me but I do need to have the same freedom as you to make decisions about money'. Not to confront would not be loving. Confrontation is not an act of blaming, but of true concern for your partner and the relationship. When it entails attacking the person of your partner or blaming him for your unmet needs, dissatisfactions and unhappiness, it ceases to be confrontation and becomes blaming. In the empathic relationship, the specific behaviour that is troubling you is the focus of confrontation. The central point about empathic relating is that the relationship with your partner is seen as paramount and is not broken because of a troublesome behaviour.

It is this issue of keeping person and behaviour separate that many partners find difficult. This is because most of us have been reared on a diet of conditional loving. When you are subjected to conditional relating, there is constant confusion between your person and your behaviour. The person of your partner is sacred and unquestionably more important than any behaviour. Furthermore, where there is unconditional love between partners, not only is the unique person of each partner valued but their relationship is also valued far beyond an annoying or difficult behaviour. Nonetheless, partners must not turn a blind eye to either their individual responsibility for correcting undesirable behaviours or their joint responsibility for engaging in actions that promote the welfare of their relationship.

The main characteristics of an empathic and unconditional relationship are set out below. Unconditional loving is a subtle and delicate matter but when it is present it has many powerful consequences. It needs also to be realised that unconditional loving is an act of will. It is easy to be loving when all is rosy in the garden of your relationship; the real test is when conflict arises.

It is clear from this list that intimacy touches all aspects of the couple's life together: emotional, social, sexual, intellectual, spiritual,

MAIN CHARACTERISTICS OF AN EMPATHIC AND UNCONDITIONAL RELATIONSHIP

- ☐ Acceptance of each other
- ☐ Demonstration of love
- ☐ Nurturance and physical caring of each other
- ☐ Non-possessive warmth and affection
- ☐ Regular affirmation of the uniqueness, worth, lovability and capability of each other
- ☐ Separation of person and behaviour
- ☐ Creation of an atmosphere of emotional safety
- ☐ Non-judgmental attitude
- ☐ Acceptance and celebration of differences between you
- ☐ Respect and value for each other
- ☐ Active listening
- ☐ An interest in each other's lives
- ☐ Sensitivity to and encouragement of each other's interests, hobbies, career, friendships and ways of doing things
- ☐ Acknowledgment of strengths and weaknesses by each of you
- ☐ Genuineness in your interactions with each other
- ☐ Couple relationship neither threatened nor broken because of differences and difficulties (except where irreconcilable differences exist)
- ☐ Active efforts to meet each other's sexual needs
- ☐ Fostering of separateness and independence of each other
- ☐ Encouragement and praise of each other's behavioural efforts
- ☐ Creating clear boundaries around the relationship
- ☐ Remembering each other's special occasions
- ☐ Direct and open communication

→

- ☐ Spontaneity
- ☐ Confrontation about behaviours that are threatening, unacceptable and invasive
- ☐ Active social life together
- ☐ Sharing of responsibilities
- ☐ Holidays together
- ☐ Companionship
- ☐ Discussion of ideas
- ☐ Acceptance of need for universal meaning and spirituality
- ☐ Regular times for reflection on progress of relationship

occupational, physical and sensual. It is also concerned with each partner's own individual life, independence and separateness from the couple relationship. The greater the strength and creativity of the individual lives of the partners, the greater the richness of their relationship with one another. Creating an intimate relationship also involves the giving of support for separation from families of origin and the creation of clear boundaries around the couple relationship.

Finally, the last suggestion above is for couples to take time off on a regular basis (say once quarterly) to review how their relationship with each other is progressing and whether any protections have been revitalised or new ones slipped in since the last review. Such reflection will ensure that the relationship stays in the direction of greater intimacy.

THE IDEAL COUPLE RELATIONSHIP

I believe you actually know what kind of relationship will benefit both you and your partner. However, your experiences in childhood, particularly those with your parents, may have made it unsafe for you to openly and unconditionally reach out for love, acceptance and freedom to be your unique self. When neither personal nor inter-personal safety is present, then necessarily and creatively individuals will protect themselves from each other until both personal and interpersonal healing occurs. Even in a mature relationship individ-uals may now and again be short-tempered, critical, blaming, insensitive and so on; however the difference between a mature relationship and a protective relationship is that, in the former, sincere and genuine apologies are a regular occurrence.

What follows is an outline of how a relationship would be were both partners high in self-esteem and providing interpersonal safety for one another so that no blocks existed to the mature, individual development of each of the partners and the develop-ment of their relationship with one another.

☐ Having an intimate relationship with self
☐ Engaging in actions and interactions that create both personal and interpersonal emotional safety
☐ Demonstrating unconditional love for your partner
☐ Living in the here and now
☐ Caringly expressing all feelings in yourself
☐ Caringly responding to all feelings in your partner
☐ Communicating openly and directly
☐ Taking responsibility for control of your own behaviour and being determined not to collude with any irresponsible behav-iour on the part of your partner
☐ Undertaking and providing the support for the actions that enhance your own and your partner's self-esteem
☐ Being able to cope, grow and move on from the inevitable differences and stresses that arise in a couple relationship

☐   Respecting, valuing, understanding and meeting the reasonable emotional, social, educational, creative, spiritual, physical, recreational, behavioural and independent needs of yourself and of your partner

If, as a prospective or as a current partner, you do not meet any one of these ideals, it is important that you try to discover what protective behaviours are operating that are blocking your mature development. These protectors have been necessary for you, but now in your intimate relationship you have the ideal opportunity to heal old wounds, let go of protectors and move towards deeper intimacy with yourself and your partner. Of course you do not need to have reached fully all the goals set out before becoming intimately involved with another: if that were the case, very few would be ready for a couple relationship. However, it is vital that you begin and continue the process of undoing protective ways of being, and that you develop acceptance of self and move towards unconditionally loving your partner. Otherwise you will remain stuck in a protective relationship that may well be repeating the unhappy or unfulfilling relationship that existed between your parents.

A great protector against having to face the sad reality of your own personal vulnerabilities and the cautious or outrageous ways you behave in a relationship is to say that these suggestions are 'pie in the sky', 'not in touch with reality' and other such rationalisations. The issue of how you are in a relationship is not one that can be ignored, and any relationship that is not open and unconditional in nature only adds to the emotional wounds of the partners involved and at a wider level to the wounds of a distressed society.